# Research, policy and advocacy in the Early Years

*Writing inspired by the achievements of Professor Anne Smith*

# Research, policy and advocacy in the Early Years

*Writing inspired by the achievements of Professor Anne Smith*

Edited by Carmen Dalli and Anne Meade

NZCER PRESS

NZCER PRESS
New Zealand Council for Educational Research
PO Box 3237
Wellington
New Zealand

www.nzcer.org.nz

© The authors 2016

ISBN 978-0-947509-19-4

No part of the publication may be copied, stored or communicated in any form by any means (paper or digital), including recording or storing in an electronic retrieval system, without the written permission of the publisher.
Education institutions that hold a current licence with Copyright Licensing New Zealand may copy from this book in strict accordance with the terms of the CLNZ Licence.

A catalogue record for this book is available from the National Library of New Zealand

Designed by Smartwork Creative Ltd

*This book is dedicated to Anne Smith,
to her legacy of hope and to her determination to
make her work count for children and families.*

# Contents

| | |
|---|---|
| **Foreword** <br> Gary B. Melton | ix |
| Chapter 1 Research, policy and advocacy in the Early Years: An introduction <br> Carmen Dalli | 1 |
| Chapter 2 The early adventures of Anne and the politics of childcare <br> Helen May | 13 |
| Chapter 3 Speaking up for infants: A sociocultural approach to advocacy <br> Jayne White and Shanee Barraclough | 25 |
| Chapter 4 Children's participation in Finnish early childhood education <br> Janniina Vlasov, Leena Turja, Anne Valpas and Eeva Hujala | 37 |
| Chapter 5 Children's rights in Aotearoa New Zealand <br> Nicola Taylor and Sarah Te One | 48 |
| Chapter 6 Assessment for learning: Promoting children's rights and social justice <br> Terry Crooks, Grace Grima and Margaret Carr | 59 |
| Chapter 7 Children's rights and social justice: An analysis of Anne B. Smith's contribution <br> Mark Henaghan | 72 |
| Chapter 8 Leaders as advocates in early childhood education: Building capacity for change through development of everyday practice <br> Joce Nuttall | 86 |
| Chapter 9 The Swedish preschool system in transition <br> Ingrid Pramling Samuelsson and Pia Williams | 96 |
| Chapter 10 Towards a holistic approach to early childhood education <br> Peter Moss | 109 |
| **Index** | 121 |

# Foreword

## Gary B. Melton

In 2009 the American Orthopsychiatric Association (Ortho) awarded one of its most prestigious honours (the Marion Langer Award) to Anne B. Smith, the New Zealand scholar in childhood studies whose work inspired the development of this book. Nearly a century old, Ortho is a venerable interdisciplinary professional association dedicated to the pursuit of mental health and social justice. The Langer Award is named after Ortho's long-time (1953–1988) executive director, a sociologist who died in 1994 at the age of 85. The award is given to recognise distinguished contributions to the enhancement of human rights and the advancement of social justice.

In presenting the Langer Award, Ortho recognised Smith for the breadth, depth and persistence of her action in support of children's rights, "for her research and advocacy to ensure that the voices of children are heard". The official citation reads as follows:

> Working both in New Zealand and in international contexts, Dr. Smith has striven to increase knowledge about children's experience in both exceptional and everyday contexts. As a center director and an international scholar, she has worked both to transform studies of childhood and to diffuse the resulting knowledge within the academy itself and in teachers' lounges, television studios, and the halls of government. Showing due respect for the dignity of both children themselves and the adults who care for them, Dr. Smith has devoted much of her career to making schools and child care centers more humane. Exploring children's own values, attitudes, and experience, she has made ground-breaking contributions to understanding the nature and implications of such a child-centered perspective. Her scholarship has extended beyond educational settings and child care to the home, the playground, the health clinic, the social service agency, the lawyer's office, the courtroom, and the policy arena.

From this citation of Smith's distinguished contributions and from reviewing her résumé, one can discern a set of exemplary activities, skills and values that taken together illustrate the characteristics of scholars who are effectively engaged in the public sphere in support of children's rights. In reviewing Smith's work one is struck first by its *breadth* and its *integration*. In particular, Smith demonstrated:

- expertise and action in both research and advocacy
- concern for children's issues in both the domestic and the international spheres
- diligence and care in basic research on children's experience within both the settings of everyday life and the specialised settings for assisting children with special needs
- diligence and care in action research intended to facilitate the application of such knowledge in the settings of childhood.

This list of attributes is remarkable in relation to the history of the university and of research, policy and practice related to children. The focus on childhood studies within the university is a relatively recent phenomenon (external institutes and field settings having led the way). When it did grow, it did so in the siloed, guild-based way that children's services themselves arose—not with a coherent, holistic view of the experience of children and the others important in their lives and of the factors shaping that view.

Most notably, developmental psychology in university departments was initially focused on the creation of pristine laboratory conditions largely isolated from the social forces, both large (macro) and small (micro), that affected children's lives and their development. Indeed, as a junior faculty member in the early 1980s I heard an eminent colleague ambivalently introduce guest lecturer Urie Bronfenbrenner, the father of ecologically oriented developmental studies (Bronfenbrenner, 1979), as a scholar who had "taken the sacred cow of developmental psychology and kicked her in the udder." Of course, children's services themselves fostered largely redundant systems with missions of treatment and care in juvenile justice, child welfare, child mental health and special education—a continuing redundancy that often seems motivated by the desire to sustain the corresponding professions and to offer multiple means of control for children who ultimately have "no place to go" (Melton, Lyons, & Spaulding, 1998).

Indeed, both the study of children (typically framed as *child development*) and the provision of children's services were, until a generation ago, almost completely devoid of efforts to understand the experience of children and families by elicitation and careful consideration of their own perspectives. By contrast, as a leader in childhood studies, Smith devoted her work to broadcasting the voices of children and their caregivers. She did so among children in general in their homes, day care centres and schools, and among children in special (but nonetheless common) circumstances (e.g. children in kinship and foster care, and children experiencing parental separation and divorce). Indeed, Smith went beyond the description of children's experience to its positive construction (with the assistance of children themselves) in the context of their *citizenship*—the theme of her (2010) Langer address.

Moreover, Smith considered the meaning of that construct across cultures, within New Zealand and beyond. She was remarkably persistent and ultimately successful in ambitious efforts to inform child policy in New Zealand, first in relation to the promotion of easily available high-quality childcare, and then in regard to the abolition of physical punishment. In the international arena, where she long built and used ties within the Childwatch International network of child research centres, Smith honed her understanding of children's rights and exhorted researchers to take child citizenship seriously. In her own words, "concern with the human rights of children is a useful moral guide to researchers, [who should view] … children as competent social actors who make choices and contribute to solving their own problems" (Smith, 2015, p. 272).

Realising that examination of children's views in isolation is unduly limited, Smith talked not only with children experiencing parental separation and divorce and children living in foster families or group homes, but also with their lawyers; and not only with children in schools but also with their teachers. She studied the behaviour management of children in the home from the perspectives of both children and parents. Equally importantly, she placed great emphasis on the communication of these findings to parents, other caregivers, practising professionals, researchers and policy makers—often a formidable task in itself.

Effective scholars on children's rights are thus not only engaged in the worlds of children in diverse cultures and diverse personal circumstances; they are also experts in the multiple empirical research methods necessary for understanding children's experience in those contexts. They appreciate the need to translate findings to the various audiences for whom they may be relevant, and to adapt communications to their various missions, concerns, forums and procedures. Such efforts are critical if potentially useful information is to reach decision makers in a timely way and in a form they can apply.

To be effective, scholars on children's rights must devote time to planning for and disseminating knowledge that influences their audiences. They must do such work strategically, with a general understanding of principles of knowledge transfer and an appreciation of the sector-specific opportunities for, and obstacles to, the delivery and use of relevant knowledge about children's circumstances (cf. Melton, 1987). So the list of attributes of effective childhood researchers, as exemplified in Smith's life and work, grows to include:

- the integration of findings of pertinent research into both pre-professional and continuing education of educators, childcare providers, recreational leaders, youth development workers, social workers, health professionals, religious leaders, lawyers, judges and other adults who work with children
- the use of the mass media, advocacy organisations and personal contacts to educate the general public (including parents and children themselves) and relevant networks about the findings of pertinent research
- the use of formal processes (e.g. courtroom and parliamentary testimony, appellate briefs and government white papers) to influence the development of child and family policy.

In the end, perhaps the most critical grounding for an effective scholar in children's rights is the firm conviction, as a matter of ethics and empathy, that children's *personhood* (Smith would probably say *citizenship*) is recognised, that its meaning is appreciated, and that its application is carefully designed and monitored:

> The most fundamental need in child policy is for due respect toward children as people. Although empirical evidence may inform specific

applications of that principle, the determination of the proper course of action is usually a matter of morality and logic grounded in a level of sensitivity that one could reasonably expect among people of good will. We need a *culture of thoughtfulness* in relations with children, as with adults, so that personhood is affirmed in all of the settings in which they live, study, worship, and play. (Melton, 2014, pp. 2,561–2,562)

So I add two more attributes defining the characteristics of effective scholars in children's rights—two more lessons from Smith's life and work:

- a grounding in scholarship on childhood and, in turn, on ethical concern for the elicitation of children's own perspective
- the direction of all such activity towards strengthened norms of humane care of children themselves and of the adults who care for them, consistent in each instance with the ethics of respect for persons.

Pursuing these goals implies not only an admirable concern for children as human beings, but also the coming together of scholars in systematic structures and processes for the thoughtful expression of such concern:

Fulfilment of … norms [of thoughtfulness] must begin, respectively, with an attitude of respect and concern for all human beings (regardless of age), an appreciation of their rights, and a commitment to humane care, manifest in a collective responsibility to ensure that the Golden Rule is applied consistently and equitably. *The final prong of this statement of duties implies the presence of a learning community in which there is (a) ongoing analysis of the requisites for the maintenance of children's sense of dignity, including the protection of their rights, and the enhancement of their well-being, (b) due care in the planning and implementation of such conditions, and (c) ongoing monitoring of the effectiveness of such activity, with modifications of plans accordingly.* By necessity, each of these steps requires attention to the care being given not only to children themselves but also to the people who are most important to them. (Melton, 2014, p. 2,562, emphasis added and citations omitted)

Such a learning community may take various forms. Perhaps the best fit is provided by conceptually grounded university-based centres and institutes. Indeed, Smith's greatest legacy may be her leadership in developing the Children's Issues Centre at the University of Otago. Thus effective scholars in children's rights are often distinguished by their prowess in leadership of groups capable of both undertaking and sustaining such work. Research for social justice for children relies on university-based interdisciplinary centres (a) to facilitate the expression of diverse perspectives, and (b) to integrate pertinent philosophical and legal analysis with empirical research in the development and implementation of child and family policy and practice.

Consideration of Smith's life and work leads me to a final attribute of scholars who are effective in making a difference for children: they pursue these activities throughout a distinguished career. When one perceives a moral imperative to increase understanding of and respect for children as persons, such activities are not just a job; they comprise a way of life. These moral signposts energise one to do whatever one can to promote and protect children's interests, wherever and whenever one can. In that regard, one statistic indicates the kind of person that Smith was: almost 40 percent of her books, chapters and articles were published in the last decade of her life, after her 'retirement' in 2006. Indeed, she continued working until her last hospitalisation. It is this dedication—in combination with a thoughtful approach, a collaborative style and an exceptional intellect—that her friends and colleagues remember and that the contributors to this book seek to emulate and teach.

## References

Bronfenbrenner, U. (1979). *The ecology of human development: Experiments by nature and design.* Cambridge, MA: Harvard University Press.

Melton, G. B. (Ed.). (1987). *Reforming the law: Impact of child development research.* New York, NY: Guilford.

Melton, G. B. (2014). "Because it's the right (or wrong) thing to do: When children's well-being is the wrong outcome". In A. Ben-Arieh, F. Casas, I. Frønes, & J. E. Korbin (Eds.), *Handbook of child well-being: Theories, methods, and policies in global perspective* (Vol. 4, pp. 2,561–2,574). Dordrecht, The Netherlands: Springer.

Melton, G. B., Lyons, P. M. Jr., & Spaulding, W. (1998). *No place to go: The civil commitment of minors*. Lincoln, NE: University of Nebraska Press.

Smith, A. B. (2010). Children as citizens and partners in strengthening communities. *American Journal of Orthopsychiatry, 80,* 103–108.

Smith, A. B. (2015). Conclusion: Challenges for research on children's rights. In A. B. Smith (Ed.), *Enhancing children's rights: Connecting research, policy, and practice* (pp. 259–273). Basingstoke, UK: Palgrave Macmillan.

# Chapter 1 Research, policy and advocacy in the Early Years: An introduction

Carmen Dalli

This book is about research, policy and advocacy in the early years. It is inspired by the work of Professor Anne B. Smith, whose influential four-decade career as a researcher and advocate for children has left an indelible impact on early-years scholarship and on right-based approaches to policy in Aotearoa New Zealand and beyond.

In this introduction Anne Meade and I, as editors, pay tribute to Anne Smith: her work and her legacy. We introduce the chapters of this volume written by colleagues, friends and past students as a way to collectively honour her through the medium that Anne Smith herself used so effectively in the service of children and their well-being: research and scholarship. We argue that research, policy and advocacy in the early years are as important today as they were throughout Anne Smith's long and distinguished career. The unique blend of research and advocacy that characterised Anne Smith's work inspires us to those principles that must never be compromised, and to ongoing dedication to bringing about necessary change when the *status quo* falls short of those principles.

## Honouring Professor Anne Smith

Professor Anne Smith's academic career in New Zealand began in 1974, when, having completed her MEd at the University of Alberta in Canada in 1969 and a PhD in 1971 as a Commonwealth Scholar, she was offered a position at the Department of Education at Otago University, where she had previously graduated with a BHSc and a BA.

Anne Meade, joint editor of this book with me, remembers first meeting Anne Smith in the year following her appointment at Otago. Anne Smith was a young academic speaking at the first early childhood convention in Christchurch in 1975. Helen May, in the second chapter of this monograph, describes why this was a very significant year for mothers and for young children. At the convention Anne Smith was on stage making "The Case for Quality Day Care in New Zealand", a case which was sub-titled, "Liberation of Children and Parents" (Smith, 1977). In the mid-seventies many resisted support for childcare because they believed it would encourage mothers to take paid jobs. Anne Smith argued differently. In a foreshadowing of a principle that was to be the foundation of much of her subsequent advocacy for quality early childhood services for children and families, she boldly argued that good childcare addresses both the rights of children and women's rights:

> there is no evidence to suggest failure to provide day care results in fewer going to work. Failure to provide good day care does, however, result in second-rate, possibly damaging care for children. (Smith, 1977 p. 248)

She concluded:

> There is growing awareness that child care is an educational and social service that is a necessity for some families ... We must, therefore, expect a greatly increased level of government support, a professionalism of child care resources, and a greater degree of co-ordination between the government departments concerned—Health, Education and Social Welfare. (p. 262)

Anne Smith's child's rights arguments in that speech turned out to lay the foundations for New Zealand becoming, in 1985, one of the first countries in the OECD[1] to integrate childcare administration into its education department, an achievement that Peter Moss comments on in the final chapter of this book.

Anne Smith's conclusions that day were prophetic. She had laid out the strategic directions for early childhood care and education policy and scholarship for the next few decades. Many of the chapters in this book speak to these strategic directions and throw light on her contributions in setting them.

The 1980s and 1990s were a time of intense activity in the New Zealand early childhood education and care (ECEC) sector, both in policy and in advocacy. Anne Smith was part of both spheres of activity, one of the coalition of women activists, unionists and academics who came together to create change and help women "gain a foot in the door" (Meade, 1990). As Helen May's chapter shows, during the 1970s Anne Smith was not only active speaking at academic and practitioner conferences but also took an energetic role in setting up the Dunedin Community Childcare Centre, using it as the site of some of her early research on children's experiences in day-care settings. In the 1980s Anne Smith's research reflected cutting-edge themes preoccupying researchers elsewhere: sex differences in children's activities (Smith, 1983; 1985); sex-role stereotyping (Smith & Grimwood, 1983; Smith & van der Vyver, 1981); and parent–staff communications in early childhood settings (Smith & Hubbard, 1988), contributing to putting these themes on the local and global pedagogical agenda as much as the research one.

During the 1990s Anne Smith's commitment to the principle that all children deserved to be in high quality early childhood settings, irrespective of the type of service they attended (Smith, 1977), became an even stronger focus of her research and advocacy, and continued to be so throughout her career (Smith, 1996a, 1996b, 2012, 2015). She was particularly passionate about provision for the youngest children, historically treated as needing 'only care' rather than education. In the late 1970s she had taken advantage of a visit by Dr Bettye Caldwell—one of the founders of Head Start in the USA and an advocate of integrated care and education provision which she referred to as "educare"—to produce

---

1 Organisation for Economic Co-operation and Development.

a film entitled *We Can't Afford to be Casual about Child Care* (Smith & Milan, 1978). The film featured Caldwell as the expert speaker and focused on explaining the message about quality ECEC to academics and policy makers, as well as to teachers and parents.

Building on this early experience, the video *Early Childhood Educare: The Search for Quality* (Smith & van der Vyver, 1993) was strategically produced to coincide with the launch of the campaign for Quality Early Childhood Education mounted by the Combined Early Childhood Union of Aotearoa. The campaign was in response to the unravelling of the Before Five (Lange, 1988) policies and had Smith as a key speaker. As another speaker and participant in the event, I remember the powerful impact of the video. To this day it remains a valuable resource—not only for its historical significance and the way that it includes cameo appearances by eminent international and national early childhood scholars, but also because of the list of 11 features of quality that became a reference point in national discussions about what parents should look for when choosing an ECEC service for their children.

The international scholars featured in the video—Professor Lilian Katz and Dr Anne Stonehouse—had been invited by Anne Smith, as chair of the programme sub-committee for the 1991 Early Childhood Convention, to be keynote speakers. Leading scholars in their field, their presence in New Zealand was an unmissable opportunity to push forward her advocacy agenda—and she used it to the full.

In 1995 Anne Smith was appointed inaugural director of the Children's Issues Centre (CIC) at Otago University. The brief of the CIC extended beyond the early years, and with it the scope of Anne's Smith's research, advocacy and policy influence. Using her formidable energy and extensive international networks, she quickly established the CIC at the cutting edge of childhood studies. In 1997 Anne Smith initiated the *Childrenz Issues* journal, which, in combination with a series of seminars hosted in different New Zealand cities, brought new awareness to issues involving children, including how to ensure children have a voice in research and in social and legal processes generally (Smith, Taylor, & Gollop, 1999, 2000); children's rights in schools; children's citizenship and nation building (Taylor & Smith, 2009); the effects of divorce and other family changes on children; and young people's participation in local government (Smith, Nairn, Sligo, Gaffney, & McCormack, 2003). In this period Anne Smith's advocacy for children's rights broadened considerably, perhaps reaching its peak in her courageous advocacy for the repeal of section 59 of the Crimes Act in 2007, which forms part of the story told by Mark Henaghan in Chapter 7 of this book.

Although Anne Smith formally retired in 2006, she remained active in speaking up for children of all ages, and in research and writing until the very end: her final piece of writing—a chapter for *The Sage Handbook of Early Childhood Policy* (Miller, Cameron, Dalli, & Barbour, in press)—was delivered to the editors just a few days before her final illness. Throughout Anne Smith's long and distinguished career no moment was wasted. Using her own research and best evidence from other scholars in New Zealand, North America, Australia and Europe to support her case, she worked tirelessly to put children 'at the centre' of her work.

Anne Smith's outstanding achievements have been recognised in many ways, including through receiving a New Zealand 1990 Commemoration Medal from the Queen; being elected fellow of the New Zealand Royal Society in 1995; an honorary doctorate from the University of Oulu in Finland in 1998; and being made a Companion of the New Zealand Order of Merit in 2007. As Gary Melton explains in the foreword to this book, the Marion Langer Award was another rare international honour bestowed on Anne Smith by the American Orthopsychiatric Association in 2009; it is awarded for distinguished contributions to the advancement of human rights and social justice. However, as her husband John Smith said shortly after his wife's death, what mattered to Anne were not the honours but the things that made children's lives better.

## *Why research, policy and advocacy?*

This volume takes its title from the three pillars of activity that formed the basis of Anne Smith's career: research, policy and advocacy. The authors have contributed chapters that illuminate the vital connection between doing and using research and policy decisions that are effective in improving the lives of children and their families and whānau. In developing their arguments from the basis of their own research, the authors have reflected on themes in Anne Smith's work, taking the opportunity to highlight different aspects of her distinct contributions in her three areas of activity. Half of the chapters focus on research, advocacy and policy in Aotearoa New Zealand, but the book is enriched by five insightful accounts from Australia, England, Sweden, Finland and the United States—countries that New Zealand looks to for new learning about early childhood education.

Today, research, policy and advocacy in the early years are as important as ever. In increasingly diverse and complex socioeconomic contexts, governments all over the world are looking at early-years education as a time of investment that will deliver results down the line. The results sought by governments vary in their details, but they are usually tied to national policy agendas for economic growth and human capital development. For governments, human beings are not only themselves the goal of human development, but also the means for achieving a country's economic development and wellbeing goals. Governments need tools to achieve their policy goals, and officials look to researchers to identify the factors associated with the successful realisation of those goals. The interplay between research and policy is well known, so advocates for new policies seek to base their arguments on research—from the academy in New Zealand and overseas, or from case studies from the community.

Such global views of the function of ECEC provisions are seldom visible in the settings where the daily lives of children unfold in the interactions they have with their educators and their holistic environment. In these settings, children's and adults' preoccupations are more demonstrably about such immediate issues as whether the morning leave-taking from the parents was difficult; a child's success or otherwise in joining peers in play; or the levels of boisterous play, or sustained interactions, that are possible within the spatial and staffing constraints and affordances of a setting.

While such day-to-day concerns might appear mundane to politicians and policy officials, in reality it is the policy settings of the characteristics of good-quality ECEC that make or break the nature of children's experiences in ECEC services. Moreover, the impacts of those experiences ripple out to affect parents and whānau, including in their workplace. Children are often positioned by politicians as mere instruments for achieving governmental goals, but this link between macro events outside of the children's control and what happens in day-to-day settings where children live their lives was never forgotten by Anne Smith.

We must heed the message to create environments in which children can thrive, advanced so courageously by Professor Anne Smith's advocacy for children and through the evidence base of her research. This book argues for taking a holistic approach to viewing children as having rights, just like any other member of society, but also as a citizen in relationship with others. Children are as affected by policy, legal and economic decisions made in organisational contexts they may never enter as they are by day-to-day events in their family, their neighbourhood, their educational or their recreational contexts. In this way, the traditional African proverb, "It takes a village to raise a child", is at the heart of the monograph.

The book starts with a foreword in which Gary Melton provides a biographical picture of Anne Smith as a globally significant figure in the field of children's rights, and in advocating for children to be treated as citizens—a picture to which this introduction adds a local flavour. Melton highlights key characteristics of Anne Smith's research and advocacy: its breadth and integration, and its impact on policy through its methodological rigour and political acumen, as well as the ability to translate research to reach multiple audiences. In the second chapter, Helen May—long-time colleague, valued friend and admirer of Anne Smith—extends this biographical picture through oral history accounts of the early part of Anne's personal and academic 'adventures'. Presenting excerpts from Anne's own telling of her life adds a uniquely personal flavour that rounds out the more academic aspects referred to in other chapters of the book.

Chapter 3 is co-authored by Jayne White and Shanee Barraclough, two of a number of ex-students whose leadership qualities Anne Smith was so good at recognising and nurturing. Established academics and advocates for children in their own right, White and Barraclough take a sociocultural perspective in arguing for the importance of taking ECEC provisions for infants seriously and what this means for societies.

In Chapter 4 a team of Finnish researchers that includes a long-time colleague of Anne Smith, Eeva Hujala, discuss how ECEC teachers in

Finland are responding to the shift of administrative responsibility for ECEC from the Ministry of Social Affairs and Health to the Ministry of Education and Culture in 2013. They outline a model for enhancing children's participation in ECEC settings. The authors argue that in the context of strong societal, legislative and curricular support for children's participation rights in ECEC, more research is required on how to inform systematic work by ECEC staff to involve children and parents in the planning and evaluation processes within ECEC programmes.

Chapters 5, 6 and 7 continue the theme of children's participation rights. In Chapter 5 Nicola Taylor and Sarah Te One, both key contributors to the local Children's Rights movement, provide an overview of the global rise of this movement, positioning Anne Smith's contribution in promoting this agenda in Aotearoa New Zealand. Key themes in their chapter are Anne Smith's advocacy for quality ECEC services and for the abolition of the physical punishment of children, a theme developed further in Chapter 7 by Mark Henaghan. Drawing on key themes in Anne Smith's final book, *Children's Rights: Towards Social Justice*, published in March 2016, Henaghan provides a legal perspective on children's rights in families, in ECEC settings, in schools, in child protection systems, in health, and in the workplace.

Taking a different focus on children's participation rights, in Chapter 6 Terry Crooks, Grace Grima and Margaret Carr pool their impressive and diverse research and policy expertise in educational assessment to articulate five principles of assessment that are consistent with principles of social justice discussed in Anne Smith's last book (Smith, 2016). Based on the premise that formative assessment is about "evoking information about learning and using that information to improve learning" (p. 68), the authors argue that their five principles are essential to achieving the purpose to which Anne Smith devoted her life's work: promoting children's rights and social justice.

The final three chapters focus on structural systems and policy, connecting to principles espoused by Anne Smith herself and to the United Nations Convention on the Rights of the Child. Taking as her entry point the role of leaders in ECEC services or settings, in Chapter 8 Joce Nuttall reflects on her research to argue that opportunities for advocacy and social change arise even in the most everyday situations.

She concludes with a call for approaches to leadership development that systematically support leaders to provide the safe, protected and healthy environments necessary for children's holistic development.

Chapter 9 outlines recent changes in the Swedish preschool system, traditionally seen as a model by many other countries, including New Zealand. Ingrid Pramling, another of Anne Smith's long-term international colleagues, and Pia Williams discuss the shift in pedagogy brought about by a rapid expansion in preschool places, the decentralisation of administration to municipalities, and population changes. They argue that the aspiration for ECEC to compensate for unequal social conditions is undermined in the absence of adequate structural support, and identify appropriate adult:child ratios and training and professional development as two key factors.

The book concludes with a reflective evaluation by Peter Moss on the care and education integrationist project across Europe, which rounds up with a comparison of ECEC policies in England and New Zealand. Moss's chapter provides a fitting end to this volume, offering a big-picture analysis that highlights both the low and the high points in the achievement of one of the most important policy goals of the New Zealand ECEC sector in the last half century—the integration of care and education into high quality ECEC services for all children. Moss's chapter ends with a salutation to Anne Smith for her role in the achievement of this goal, and for "offering hope that alternatives exist and showing that they can be realised" (p. 119).

This book is dedicated to Anne Smith, to her legacy of hope and to her determination to make her work count for children and families.

## References

Lange, D. (1988). *Before Five: Early childhood care and education in New Zealand*. Wellington: Department of Education.

Meade, A. (1990). Women and children gain a foot in the door. *New Zealand Women's Studies Journal*, 6(1). 96–111.

Miller, L., Cameron, C., Dalli, C., & Barbour, N. (Eds.) (in press). *The Sage Handbook of Early Childhood Policy*. London, UK Sage.

Smith, A. B. (1977). The case for quality day care in New Zealand: liberation of children and parents. In B. O'Rourke & J. Clough (Eds.), *Early childhood in New Zealand*. Auckland: Heinemann.

Smith, A. B. (1983). Sex differences in activities in early childhood centres. *New Zealand Journal of Psychology, 12*(2): 74–81.

Smith, A. B. (1985). Teacher modelling and sextyped play preferences. *New Zealand Journal of Educational Studies, 20*(1): 39–47.

Smith, A. B. (1996a). The quality of childcare centres for infants in New Zealand, in *New Zealand Association for Research in Education State-of-the-Art Monograph No 4*. Palmerston North: Massey University.

Smith, A. B. (1996b). Early childhood educare: Quality programmes which care and educate. *Childhood Education—International Perspectives. 72*(6), 330–335.

Smith, A. B. (2012). A good start for all children: the case for universal, accessible, high quality early childhood education. *Children,* Winter (81), 22–26.

Smith, A. B. (2015). Can home-based care offer high quality early childhood education? *New Zealand Journal of Educational Studies, 50*(1), 71–85.

Smith, A. B. (2016). Children's Rights. Towards Social Justice. New York, USA: Momentum Press.

Smith, A. B., & Grimwood, S. (1983). Sex role stereotyping and children's concepts of teachers and principals. *Australian Journal of Early Childhood, 8*(2): 23–28.

Smith, A. B. & Hubbard, P. M. (1988). Staff/parent communication in Early Childhood Centres. *New Zealand Journal of Educational Studies, 23*(2): 175–199.

Smith, A. B., & Milan, B. M. (1978). *We can't afford to be casual about child care.* [16 mm film, 28 min.] Dunedin: Audio Visual Production Centre / Department of Education, University of Otago. https://unitube.otago.ac.nz/view?m=EhyF8JEXjbB

Smith, A. B., Nairn, K., Sligo, J., Gaffney, M., & McCormack, J. (2003). *Case studies of young people's participation in public life: Local government, boards of trustees and the youth parliament.* Dunedin: Children's Issues Centre.

Smith, A. B., Taylor, N. J., & Gollop, M. M. (1999). Children's voices in foster or kinship care: knowledge, understanding and participation. *Journal of Child Centred Practice, 6*(1), 9–37.

Smith, A. B., Taylor, N. J. & Gollop, M. (2000). (Eds.). *Children's voices: Research, policy and practice.* Auckland: Pearson Education.

Smith, A. B., & van der Vyver, R. (1981). *Blue for a girl: Sex roles in early childhood* [16 mm film, 40 min.] Dunedin: HEDC/Department of Education, University of Otago.

Smith, A. B. & van der Vyver, R. (1993). *Early childhood educare: The search for quality.* [Videotape, 38 mins]. Dunedin: Education Department and Audio Visual Production Centre, University of Otago. https://unitube.otago.ac.nz/view?m=1cxL8JFEiTk

Taylor, N., & Smith, A .B. (Eds.). (2009). *Children as citizens?: International voices.* Dunedin: Otago University Press.

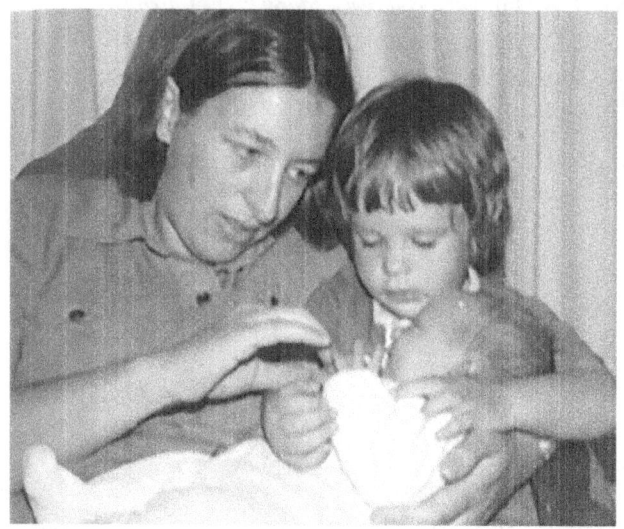

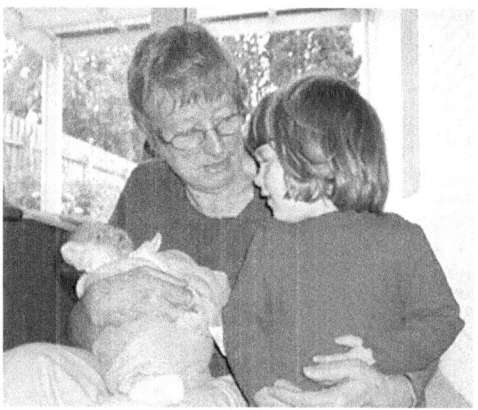

Top: Anne, Catherine and Juliet, June 1972

Middle left: Juliet, Anne and Catherine, North Temple Valley, summer 1978

Middle right: Catherine, Anne, Juliet and John, Holyford Road end, Easter 1981

Bottom: Tomas (grandson), Anne, Jessica (granddaughter), 2003

*Photo source: John Smith*

# Chapter 2  The early adventures of Anne and the politics of childcare

Helen May

## *Introduction*

Dr Anne Smith returned to New Zealand in late 1974 with her husband, John, and two preschool children, after studying and working in Canada. Anne had been appointed to the University of Otago as a lecturer in education in the field of human development. The 1970s was a turning point in the history of early childhood education. Unlike the established, popular and part day preschool services of kindergarten and playcentres supported by the Department of Education, childcare services were sidelined under an umbrella of welfare and tainted by both public and political disapproval. During this decade advocates for childcare made new alliances and started to gain political attention. Anne's return to New Zealand unexpectedly coincided with these times and dramatically altered the course of her intended academic career.

In Canada, where both Anne and John had been studying for their doctorates as well as teaching, they had used various childcare arrangements. For a time Anne was also on the governance board of a centre, which in an interview with the author she described as "when I started to understand the more detailed texture of what a good childcare centre was like".[1] There were federal government subsidies for childcare in Canada, which was not the case in New Zealand: "It was a pretty bad scene in Dunedin". There was a dearth of provision, no funding support and little understanding of what comprised quality childcare:

> The university crèche had this philosophy that the shorter the time you left the child the better. They were good people who were trying to do a good job, but it was like a railway station. There were kids and parents coming and going. There was no settled programme. I did not feel comfortable leaving a child in something like that all day. I did have something to do with the crèche later, and tried to tell them that it's not true that the shorter the time you left the child the better. It's very unsettling for them.[2]

Back in New Zealand, Anne and John cobbled together various childcare arrangements, including kindergarten and a home carer. However, when John got a position at Dunedin Teachers' College and Anne continued working at Otago University, it was made clear to Anne that not only should she stay at home with her children but she should also put her husband's career first. "It was quite clear that this was not what people did here."[3] Likewise, within the Department of Education at the university there was strong support for John Bowlby's theories on the ills of maternal deprivation (Bowlby, 1951), with several colleagues active in organisations opposing childcare.

Thus began Anne's adventurous journey over more than four decades using the personal and institutional resources of academia, through research, writing, presentation, conferencing, film making and travel, to present the research and policy arguments for quality childcare and, more broadly, for quality experiences in early childhood. Framed around the year 1975, and its aftermath, this chapter details some of the events, people and politics encountered by Anne in her first ventures as an academic into the New Zealand early childhood scene. This is recalled as a pivotal year for the politics of childcare with the

---

[1] Interview with Anne Smith, 1994.
[2] Ibid.
[3] Ibid.

crafting of some shared understanding of the equity issues for women and children (May, 2003, 2009).

## *International Women's Year: The conference circuit*

Soon after arriving in New Zealand, Anne was in the midst of a flurry of conferences, reports and submissions. 1975 was International Women's Year (IWY), and a select committee was established by Parliament to consider 'the extent of discrimination of women in New Zealand'. Its report gave considerable focus to childcare, 'accept[ing] the principle that for women to be able to achieve genuine choice in their lives some of the responsibility for the care of the young must be borne by the wider community' (Select Committee on Women's Rights, 1975, p. 86). Rosslyn Noonan was appointed IWY national organiser and became a key player in early childhood politics over subsequent years. She recalled:

> 1975 is the crucial year because it brought together early childhood education and the women's movement which had overlapping issues … Early childhood education people were beginning to analyse their inability to deliver what they saw as incredibly important—equality for all children … A number of us who were in that first wave of feminists also had young children. We knew about suburban neurosis … The issues I was involved with [during 1975] were … focusing on gaining a healthier community which supported families with young children. I don't think we succeeded.[4]

In the aftermath of the IWY United Women's Convention, the headline in the *Sunday Times* (19 October 1975) read "Childcare Unites Women". The article named many organisations that were agreed that a united front was called for:

> The National Council of Women has been trying for over a year to talk with Government about childcare … 'We get nice answers from them about what they've done and what they're doing, but their overall commitment seems lacking.'

Several government-sponsored conferences followed in the aftermath. Anne was in attendance:

---

4  Interview with Rosslyn Noonan, 1999.

One of the first things I did was give a paper at the first Early Childhood Convention in Christchurch in 1975. It was called 'The Case for Quality Day Care—Liberation of Children and Parents' ... There wasn't a single other thing about childcare at the conference. It was very kindergarten dominated![5]

Anne assured her audience that 'The development of quality day care programmes is not a challenge to the family ... Daycare is ... an additional means of support [and] may actually improve or enhance the quality of family life' (Smith, 1978, p. 248). To support her argument Anne cited research indicating that childcare could be beneficial for children (Caldwell, 1967; Fein & Clarke-Stewart, 1973). She also cited Michael Rutter in his book *Maternal Deprivation Reassessed* (1972, p. 64):

> Day care need not necessarily interfere with the normal mother–child attachment and the available evidence gives no reason to suppose that the use of day nurseries has any long-term psychological or physical ill effects.

Anne's favoured model was community childcare, with parent involvement and professional support from qualified teachers, 'which should be provided regardless of the family's ability to pay for it' and for which one 'must therefore expect a greatly increased level of government support' (Smith, 1978, pp. 251–252).

There were over a thousand attendees at this first early childhood convention. The Director-General of Education, William Renwick, addressed delegates on the theme of the 'moving frontier' in early childhood education and summed up the childcare issue thus:

> Most of us who have thought about early childhood education find the circumstances of these parents so foreign to our experiences, and the situation of their children so fraught with the possibilities of damage, that we are ill-equipped to find satisfactory educational answers to the problems they pose.

He posed a challenge to the mainly kindergarten and playcentre audience:

> We have to break the mould of our own convictions and attitudes before we can begin to think constructively about finding solutions

---

5  Interview with Anne Smith, 1994.

to situations as they are, not as we would like them to be. (Renwick, 1978, p. 235)

Government's response to the 'moving frontier' was slow, but Renwick's address signalled that new policy directions were needed. He also noted the emergence of a 'national constituency' for early childhood. The members of this constituency, of which Anne was to become a key player, found the translation of changing attitudes into policies frustratingly slow.

Anne also attended the 1975 Education and the Equality of the Sexes Conference, meeting with other key players such as Geraldine McDonald, Beverley Morris, Marie Bell, Val Burns, Wendy Lee, Anne Meade and Rosslyn Noonan. Not surprisingly, the headlines in the conference proceedings stated, "Early Childhood Education: An Angry Group". Their report addressed the status of early childhood services in the education sector. Noonan wrote:

> An analysis of the staffing structure of early childhood educational services revealed a disproportionate number of women at the bottom and an equally disproportionate number of men at the top. The workers are almost exclusively female, the consumers are children and their families, and [the] decision-makers [are] men. (Department of Education, 1976, p. 7)

Anne's 1975 political conference circuit wound up in November at the annual conference of the New Zealand Association of Child Care Centres (NZACCC), an organisation founded by Sonja Davies in 1963.[6] The NZACCC had been a lonely political voice for government funding support for centres and qualifications for staff. In 1975 the organisation found itself amidst a tide of support from various women's organisations, including key people across the early childhood world (May, 2003).

Norah Fryer was also attending her first conference. In Christchurch she was involved in setting up a centre at the Christchurch Technical Institute.

---

6 This organisation has had various name changes: New Zealand Childcare Association, with the later addition of the Māori name Te Tari Puna Ora o Aotearoa, and then in 2015 this was changed to Te Rito Maioho—Early Childhood New Zealand.

My lasting memory is of Anne Smith and her dream of wanting a recognised qualification for anyone who worked with children. Anne gave us this beautiful dream of what she would like in her 10-year plan for childcare. I can remember being a bit apprehensive and saying, 'That sounds wonderful, but what can I take back to the people in Christchurch to do today?' From there I got involved in the training committee [as did Anne].[7]

Both Anne and Norah Fryer were subsequently elected to the NZACCC executive. Not waiting for government to establish a qualification in childcare, the organisation had established its own field-based training, funded in its early years through lottery grants and voluntary tutors. Anne Smith's involvement lent considerable academic respectability to the idea of childcare training.

## International Women's Year: Establishing a childcare centre

Anne's attendance at the NZACCC conference had been at the invitation of colleagues she had met on the Dunedin home front: Pat Hubbard and Phyllis Levitt, both of whom had some international experience of childcare. All three women were members of the Dunedin Collective for Women, for whom issues concerning women and childcare were high on the agenda. This was the origin of the Dunedin Community Childcare Centre, the foundation centre of the Dunedin Community Childcare Association which celebrated its 40th jubilee in 2015. The Women's Collective attended an IWY Committee meeting in Dunedin:

> We knew there was government money for International Women's Year and so we decided to break through this seemingly impossible barrier of how did you get started. We applied and became Dunedin's project for IWY. The temerity of it! Fairly amazing really![8]

---

7   Interview with Norah Fryer, 2003.
8   Interview with Pat Hubbard, 1994.

Dr Anne Smith and the Rev. Ewing Stevens, 24 July 1975, *Evening Star*

In the event there was a groundswell of community support. Ewing Stevens, a charismatic Methodist Minister, chaired the establishment committee. Anne recalled:

> He was extremely good at getting the public on side. It was amazing. We held a public meeting and there were 250 people there. That was quite extraordinary to get 250 people out to a public meeting. He used to talk on the radio, and he pulled those people in, including a number of prominent men, but we did most of the donkey-work.[9]

There was much debate about the centre's philosophy and operational practices:

> We wanted it to be for everyone, but it was more of a feminist thing for women who wanted or had to work. We also had quality principles that we wanted too. We had some ideals about it being for children too … We talked about parent involvement. We would use

---

9   Interview with Anne Smith, 1994.

psychology to plan an environment that we felt was good for kids. We were talking about training and ratios and paying the staff properly. We believed that we should have quality for the staff as well. That was the most difficult in the long run, because there was virtually nothing by way of government subsidy. [10]

Pat Hubbard was appointed the first director of the centre. In accord with its feminist origins the parents and management chose not to fund raise:

> We were really committed against it. We didn't run raffles or run cake stalls or any of those sorts of things. We just appealed for money. We discovered all the politicians … I spoke to lots of meetings as part of IWY and the whole education process. I remember a few appalling meetings of men's organisations where it became clear that the threat was that their wives might want to use the centre. One man became absolutely enraged.[11]

Feminist principles also shaped the programme:

> The non-sexist programme we tried to run was very important from the beginning because of IWY and feminism. I had long talks with Marie Bell who was on a committee for producing non-sexist books. Marie was one of the earliest official visitors.[12]

The new centre struggled for survival in a policy context that was not inclusive of childcare, but it also flourished as a site of community activism, support for parents, feminist endeavour, and engagement with the latest ideas on quality early childhood practice. Not surprisingly, the centre became the site of Anne's first research forays into early childhood (Smith, 1980). She summed up the experience as "really quite exciting because it got me involved in the national politics of childcare but it also shaped my academic work. My own children never benefited from that project, but my work, no doubt, did."[13]

---

10   Interview with Anne Smith, 1994.
11   Interview with Pat Hubbard, 1994.
12   Interview with Pat Hubbard, 1994.
13   Interview with Anne Smith, 1994.

## In the aftermath of 1975

International Women's Year was followed in 1976 by the Prime Minister's Conference on Women in Social and Economic Development. Continuing the momentum, the conference addressed the need for a national childcare policy (Committee on Women, 1976a, 1976b). The 'Women and the Care of Children syndicate' at the conference was led by Geraldine McDonald and Rosslyn Noonan. A position paper, *Childcare: Facts, Principles and Problems*, was prepared by the Government's Committee on Women. The key statement was:

> Whether or not a mother should go out to work or remain at home to care for her children is a decision to be made by the woman concerned … She should ideally be able to make a free choice between the two … the lack of adequate child care centres means that a mother does not really have a free choice between working in the home and in paid employment. (Committee on Women, 1976, p. 8)

What had emerged was a group of women who were now orchestrating a campaign that positioned early childhood issues in relation to the role of women on the political agenda. Anne summed up the mood:

> It brought together a diverse group of women from all over the country. The fact that we were able to get close to a consensus was influential. This link of feminism with early childhood was very important, because I didn't see it happening overseas where early childhood people had this very nice image, and they wouldn't be too loud. Yet in New Zealand these people were deciding to speak with a clear voice. They began saying that this is important work women are doing that isn't valued, and it isn't getting nearly as much funding as other levels in the education system. We began to get what Anne Meade has called 'a cumulative discourse'. I know the origin of the childcare movement went back to Sonja Davies in the 1960s, but the mid-1970s brought it together.[14]

In 1977, with both Anne and Pat Hubbard on the Executive, and at the behest of Anne, the NZACCC sponsored Bettye Caldwell's visit to New Zealand. Caldwell was a high-profile advocate of the benefits

---

14 Interview with Anne Smith, 1994.

of quality childcare (Caldwell, 1967, 1972). She had established the first federally funded infant daycare programme at the University of Syracuse, New York, as a research project funded under Head Start. The programme operated for economically deprived infants and their mothers, and successfully demonstrated benefits for the children and their families (Caldwell, 1967). It also demonstrated what a quality daycare programme for infants and toddlers might mean in terms of a curriculum for children and a training programme for adults (Honig & Lally, 1972). Caldwell's visit was a boost for childcare advocates and activists. Framed around an interview with Caldwell, in 1978 Anne undertook her first film production, *You Can't Afford to be Casual about Childcare*. Against the backdrop of the new Dunedin centre, Caldwell is featured telling prospective parents what to look for in selecting a childcare centre, and assures them that a quality centre will be beneficial for their children.

Caldwell worked hard during her tour of New Zealand, visiting the Ministers of Education and Social Welfare, appearing on television and radio, and addressing meetings. University academics were keen to arrange meetings, and Caldwell's visit demonstrated that opinion had shifted, even if the political will for change was slow. The NZACCC paid tribute to her for the support she gave them in dispelling the myths of childcare particularly around the ills of maternal deprivation (Bowlby, 1951). As Caldwell stated:

> In any field of endeavour a set of myths and beliefs can develop, which, in time, are reacted to as though they are hard core facts. How can we in early childhood protect children and ourselves from the effects of premature and over-zealous espousal of inadequately tested ideas? (Caldwell, cited in Lamb, 1978)

Meanwhile, progress on the political front was tortuous. Recommendation 32 from the 1976 Conference on Women in Social and Economic Development had asked the Minister of State Services

> to arrange as a matter of priority for the State Services Commission to take all necessary steps in consulting [list of Government Departments] … to devise an effective administration for policies relating to early childhood care and education. That in doing this there be full consultation with women's organisations, municipal

authorities and interested voluntary organisations with a view to rationalising local provision of early childhood care and education within a national framework. (Committee on Women, 1976b, p. 17)

Thus began a long saga, told elsewhere (McDonald, 1981), of the State Services Commission's report *Early Childhood Care and Education* (1980), which was eventually released in 1981 then shelved by a National Government in 1982. It is a tribute to the tenacious guardianship of Geraldine McDonald that the report emerged in the form it did. The recommendations were that

- there be three early childhood services [playcentre, kindergarten and childcare] with administrative responsibility in the Department of Education
- there be 'equitable' funding for childcare and that this be based not on the 'welfare' principle but on the principle of a contribution to a recognised service
- the government subsidise up to 50 percent of the cost to parents.

The shelving of these recommendations caused an outcry of frustration by childcare advocates, as exemplified by Anne in a letter to the *NZ Listener* (18 September 1982):

[I]t is hard to accept that all the patient restrained work since the early 1970s is to be set aside; that all the 'expert' and grass roots support, reports and recommendations are to be ignored.

This crisis ends the first instalment of the 'adventures of Anne'. We know now that the State Services Commission report was a watershed in the politics of childcare and an iconic example of advocacy. The report acknowledged the benefits of childcare for families and society and proposed a policy framework for including childcare within the education sector. The recommendations subsequently spearheaded the rollercoaster initiatives of the 1984–1990 Labour Government. All of the women named above were key players in the journey, which is still underway.

## References

Bowlby, J. (1951). *Maternal care and mental health.* Geneva: World Health Organisation.

Caldwell, B. (1967). What is the optimal learning environment for the young child? *American Journal of Orthopsychiatry, 37,* 8–22.

Caldwell, B. (1972). *Can young children have a quality life in daycare?* Foundation lecture presented at Pacific Oaks College, Pasadena, California.

Committee on Women. (1976a). *Child-care: Facts, principles and problems.* IWY76-Synd 2-1. Women in Social and Economic Development Conference, Wellington: Author

Committee on Women. (1976b). *Report of Conference on Women and Social and Economic Development.* Wellington: Author

Department of Education. (1976). *A report on the National Conference in International Women's Year 1975, Education and the Equality of the Sexes.* Wellington: Author.

Fein, G. G., & Clarke-Stewart, A. (1973). *Daycare in context.* London, UK: Wiley and Sons.

Honig, A. S., & Lally, J. R. (1972). *Infant caregiving: A design for training.* New York, NY: Syracuse University Press.

Lamb, M. (1978). A message from the president. *Early Childhood Quarterly, 1*(4), 1–4.

May, H. (2003). *Concerning women considering children: Battles of the Childcare Association, 1963–2003.* Wellington: Te Tari Puna Ora o Aotearoa—NZCA.

May, H. (2009). *Politics in the playground: The world of early childhood in New Zealand* (2nd ed.). Dunedin: University of Otago Press.

McDonald, G. (1981). The story of a recommendation about early childhood care and education. In M. Clark (Ed.), *The politics of education in New Zealand.* Wellington: New Zealand Council for Educational Research.

Rutter, M. (1972). *Maternal deprivation reassessed.* London: Penguin.

Select Committee on Women's Rights. (1975). *The role of women in New Zealand society.* Wellington: Government Printer.

Smith, A. (1978). The case for quality day care in New Zealand: Liberation of children and parents. In B. O'Rourke & J. Clough (Eds.), *Early childhood in New Zealand.* Auckland: Heinemann Educational Books.

Smith, A. B. (1980). A community child care scheme in New Zealand. *Australian Journal of Early Childhood, 5*(2), 26–31.

State Services Commission Working Group. (1980). *Early childhood care and education.* Wellington: Government Printer.

# Chapter 3  Speaking up for infants: A sociocultural approach to advocacy

Jayne White and Shanee Barraclough

## Introduction

Taking a sociocultural approach to the advocacy of infants involves recognising the social, cultural and historical contexts of their lived experience and therefore paying attention to the people, places and things that shape their lives. Based on the inspiration of sociocultural scholars who highlight the role of the adult in such matters, advocacy can be viewed as extending beyond the exclusive domain of individual families by implicating wider society in the education and care of our youngest. A sociocultural approach to such advocacy recognises the task for all citizens in advancing high-quality early childhood education experiences as a human rights—and more particularly a children's rights—imperative.

In this chapter the advocacy roles played by Anne Smith in speaking up for infants across pedagogical, curriculum, theoretical and political spaces are discussed in order to highlight the importance of her work for New Zealand society and, indeed, the world, in relation to a quality agenda for early childhood education (ECE). In particular, we draw on and showcase the significant body of work she conducted in collaboration with her research teams during the 1990s and as part of the initiation of the Children's Issues Centre. We argue for the enduring importance of this work because of its attention to sociocultural contexts and its key finding of the necessity of particular structural and dynamic factors in developing quality early ECE for infants. Finally, we consider the impact of her legacy on current research and policy on infants in ECE in New Zealand and conclude with what we see as the necessity of continuing with a sociocultural advocacy agenda in speaking up for the rights of infants in ECE.

## Background

Speaking up for infants in education has never been as important as it is today. Infants are now the fastest growth population for ECE service enrolments in New Zealand, and indeed globally (OECD, 2015). From a sociocultural standpoint (Rogoff, 2003), the presence of infants in ECE services can be seen as a cultural phenomenon, raising important questions about how infants' participation rights in communities are to be understood. In New Zealand the early education curriculum, *Te Whāriki* (Ministry of Education, 1996), positions infants as competent, capable learners who are able to make a valued contribution to society—now and in the future. This image of infants as contributors in their centres and communities implies the infants' capacity to speak up for themselves, be agentic partners and have their own 'voice'. Yet, as Eva Johansson (2011) has pointed out, this emphasis on competency should not overshadow the fact that infants are simultaneously vulnerable. In contemporary ECE service settings, where infants share their lives with teachers as much as their home adults, consideration of infants as simultaneously competent and vulnerable must take account of the sociocultural tenet that individuals are influenced through their "changing participation in the sociocultural activities of their communities, which also changes" (Rogoff, 2003, p. 11).

A sociocultural perspective gives prominence to the changing and connected features of child development and to the functions and goals of participation in a cultural community. By deeming infants to already be 'participants', attention is shifted away from the more traditional question of whether they ought to be participating in out-of-home settings, instead accepting the lived reality of early childhood education as a cultural activity in time and space. From this viewpoint, all members of a community have some responsibility for infants' cultural experiences and their development—including a responsibility to advocate for children as full participants in the life of their community. By extension, this includes a further responsibility to advocate for the policies and practices that affect the people, places and things in the community.

In this chapter we argue that a sociocultural approach to advocacy must respond to the inherent challenges that arise when children's rights to participate in high-quality ECE are brought into the conversation along with such global and local dynamics as economic constraints. Combined with a human rights perspective—as articulated in the United Nations Convention on the Rights of the Child (UNCRC)—a sociocultural approach to advocacy would assert the importance of interpersonal relationships for infant learning and place emphasis on the associated obligations of any education provider to provide (among other things) universal provision for "The development of the child's personality, talents and mental and physical abilities to their fullest potential" (Article 29:b) in consideration of the wishes of their parents (29:c), and as preparation for "a responsible life in a free society" (29:d). From a social justice perspective, infant participation in ECE services can play a key role in overcoming adversity, reducing inequality and setting them on the road to a 'good life'. This means that adults not only need to understand what constitutes a quality ECE service experience, but also act to ensure this is accessible to all who participate in ECE services.

Our sociocultural approach to advocacy draws inspiration from the work of Anne Smith, who made speaking up for infants in New Zealand ECE services a key focus of her research agenda. A staunch advocate for children's voices to be heard, and for adults to acknowledge their responsibilities to respond to their needs, Smith set in motion a policy agenda for New Zealand that prioritised infant learners and their families, alongside their rights to quality ECE services. Inspired by her legacy, we call for a continued research agenda concerning infant participation in ECE services in order to understand how certain educative practices achieve their intended goals or generate different ones. We suggest that research and practice that focus on infants' participation in ECE services must first and foremost seek to understand this growing phenomenon and what it means for infants, their families and those who work alongside them.

## Children's rights: Advocacy and research agendas

Anne Smith was a protagonist in the field of children's rights, pioneering a socioculturally oriented approach to advocacy for infants. Her advocacy drew on UNCRC and set a course for national accountability concerning the rights of all children to high-quality education (see also Taylor and Te One, this volume). Smith (2015) argued convincingly for a holistic response to these rights, and the positive impacts for all when these rights are addressed. Importantly, she suggested that such rights are only afforded infants when countries are serious about their obligations and put policies in place to achieve them in a sensitive manner.

From her earliest years as a New Zealand academic, and as a parent, Smith started an advocacy agenda for the participation rights of children and families in high-quality ECE services. Her involvement in establishing the Dunedin Community Childcare Association to provide ECE services for her own and other families contributed greatly to her professional commitment to national policy development concerning infants, toddlers and young children.

## Children's Issue Centre research on quality ECE for infants

In the mid-1990s Smith was instrumental in establishing the interdisciplinary Children's Issues Centre, under the auspices of Otago University. The centre is a place where children's rights are given the highest priority. Emphasis has always been firmly on motivating those working with children to maintain vigilance concerning UNCRC, including government commitments to UNCRC. The centre quickly became, and continues to be, a unique site of innovation in the field of childhood studies.

The 1990s were an important time in the history of New Zealand ECE, not least as a result of the development of *Te Whāriki* (Ministry of Education, 1996), which was the first curriculum worldwide to include infants and toddlers in its remit (White & Mika, 2013). *Te Whāriki* emphasised both *process* as well as *structural* aspects of quality provision (Dalli & White, 2016). This dual focus was helpful in New Zealand investigations of infant care and education, and for advocacy for policy changes.

The 1990s also saw one of the earliest New Zealand studies to research the quality of ECE services for infants (hereafter called the Infant Study). Led by Smith (1996b), the study examined aspects of process and structural quality in 100 ECE services in four locations and the experiences of 200 infants within them. A key finding was that the quality of infant experience in ECE was directly affected by the educators who worked with them. The value given to teaching work (qualifications, pay and working conditions) was found to be central to encounters between adults and infants. This finding established a social and economic human capital argument for government investment in quality ECE; alongside similar findings in the USA (Whitebook, Howes, & Phillips, 1989), it provided evidential leverage to argue for qualified professionals in ECE for infants as well as older children.

Supplementary analyses of the data from the Infant Study challenged the neoliberal assertion that parental choice could be a viable mechanism for improving quality care for infants (Barraclough, 1994; Barraclough & Smith, 1996; Smith & Barraclough, 1997). These analyses showed the complexity of interacting factors influencing the choice parents make for ECE of their infants. The researchers asked, "What, if any, relationships exist between the socioeconomic status, education, and income of parents and research-based measures of quality of the care?" In addition, the exploration of parents' satisfaction with the quality of their infant's centre clearly showed parents reported being satisfied, regardless of structural measures of quality or skilled observers' assessments of quality. One outcome from this study was the emergence of another advocacy agenda: for government policies that actively work to promote and increase research-informed quality group care for infants.

It is relevant to note at this point that academics were by no means asserting that the definition of 'quality' in ECE was settled. Rather, a consensus developed that objective and subjective measures of quality could not be separated. Moreover, quality ECE should be defined in the light of cultural goals and values that are negotiated from the perspective of various stakeholders, including children (Smith, 1996a).

The debates about quality continue today, with assertions that we are now 'beyond' quality (see, for example, Moss, 2008). What was raised 20 years ago, and continues today, is the point that quality is by no means a universal construct (e.g. Dalli et al., 2011). Nevertheless, there was significant evidence by the 1980s that some key features in ECE generate positive outcomes for infants: responsive interactions, safety and loving care for process quality; and qualified educators, group size and ratios for structural quality (see, e.g., Whitebook et al., 1989).

A further outcome of the Infant Study was a paper on the relationship between qualified teachers, group size and teacher–infant joint attention episodes, in which Smith argued convincingly that positive language models and shared meaning were central variables in infant learning and development, and central to infant pedagogy (Smith, 1999). The importance of pedagogy that emphasises joint attention between teachers and young children has since been corroborated in England and elsewhere (e.g. the EPPE project; Sylva et al., 2003). In this regard, as with many of her other ideas, Smith was well ahead of her time.

Subsequent analysis of the running-record observational data in the Infant Study drew attention to a different sort of pedagogical competence (Smith, Barraclough, & Sutcliffe, 1996; Smith & Barraclough, 1999). Infants and toddlers were observed engaging in conflictual episodes, which were interpreted by the research team as active social exchanges. Drawing on Vygotsky's sociocultural theory, the researchers highlighted the essential role of trained educators in recognising and responding to 'conflict' as social and emotional play and learning. These insights motivated Smith to instigate a new study with 30 early childhood teachers to ascertain their perspectives on children's aggression, conflicts and rough-and-tumble play. That study (Smith et al., 1996) found that when and how to intervene in children's peer interactions was clearly an issue needing considerable professional judgement, requiring staff to be knowledgeable and working in conditions that allowed them to notice what was going on.

With her ever-present focus on the connection between the micro-practices of early educators and macro-policy contexts, Smith noted that conditions of work in centres were part of the quality equation—good conditions of work, including appropriate ratios and small groups of children, discouraged staff turnover, and stable staff teams were able to develop effective ways of turning young children's conflict into learning. These combined findings provided further evidence for the need for ECE conditions to adhere to the agenda set out by UNCRC to enable "the development of the child's personality, talents and mental and physical abilities to their fullest potential" (Article 29:b).

## *Current research on infants in ECE in New Zealand*

The structural and dynamic features of quality and their sociocultural location in society—both central to Smith's research advocacy—continue to play a vital role in infant research. In New Zealand these are now manifested in policy documents, evaluation indicators and professional guidelines that orient quality practice. Internationally a sociocultural view of quality remains influential. As Dalli and White (2016) point out,

> the past few years have witnessed both an increasing acceptance that indicators of quality have a role to play in policy and accountability discourses, as well as a mounting acceptance of the need to revise, reconceptualise, diversify and challenge existing indicators of quality in response to local contexts and populations. (p. 39)

A flurry of commissioned reports seeking to identify policy priorities to ensure quality ECE services for infants—both in New Zealand (Dalli, White, et al., 2011) and overseas (e.g. Mathers, Eisenstadt, Sylva, Soukakou, & Ereky-Severs, 2014; Rayna, 2010; Stephen, Dunlop, & Trevarthern, 2003) reiterate this message, noting also that quality ECE for infants has lasting repercussions for society and therefore should be seen as an important investment for any country. The advocacy role set out for teachers, communities and policy makers is now well entrenched, if not always enacted.

Contemporary research has also taken up the strong pedagogical agenda that emphasises the dynamic features of intersubjective relationships. Cross-disciplinary research from neuroscience and psychology, in particular, has established an even more compelling agenda for increased attention to relationships in ECE services (Dalli & White, 2016), with quality interactions between infants and others in

ECE services now identified as an urgent priority for research globally (White & Dalli, 2017).

Associated attempts to understand the interpersonal experiences of infants in ECE services have resulted in a series of innovative new research approaches (Johansson & White, 2011; Li, Quinones, & Ridgway, in press; White & Dalli, 2017). Using video as a central means of insight, several studies have sought to delve deeply into the ways infants participate in their own learning, both in New Zealand (Dalli, Rockel et al., 2011; White, 2016a) and elsewhere (Johansson & White, 2011; Ridgway, Liang, & Quinones, 2016). Many include the perspectives of teachers, families and infants themselves (White, 2016b); while others emphasise the pedagogical and theoretical spaces that underpin practice (Harrison & Sumsion, 2014). Taken together, research of this nature realigns the subtle yet pivotal relationships that exist between structural and dynamic features of quality, which together orient the extent to which infants can participate effectively in ECE services:

> there are implications for other structural features such as group size, size of the wider environment to afford intimate yet widely visible spaces, alongside systems that support and nurture intimate relationships that are so clearly influential for infant engagement with people, places and things. These are other 'silent' aspects of the pedagogical encounter raised behind the scene. (White & Redder, 2015, p. 15)

## *Looking ahead*

Quality features—comprising structural and dynamic features—are now widely viewed as offering important standards for infants all over the world (Dalli & White, 2016). Sadly, at the time of writing, in New Zealand these are not yet set at a high level, with New Zealand ECE regulations asserting minimum standards for practice. A recent survey (White, Peter, & Ranger, in press) found that many ECE services believe that minimum standards are insufficient and are offering higher ratios and more qualified staff for under-3-year-olds than are funded by government subsidies. These services explained that their compliance to higher standards than those mandated by regulations comes at a cost. They described their commitment to optimal teacher–infant relationships within groups, to good ratios, to small groups of children, and to qualified staff who understand the importance of intersubjective experiences for infants. These survey results highlight the fact that teachers who see themselves as advocates are not merely concerned with ensuring that certain 'minimum' standards are in place; they were also speaking out for families, communities and the profession, all in the interests of high-quality ECEC (early childhood education and care) for infants. From a sociocultural advocacy framework, these results are another example of the negotiated nature of quality.

The issues raised through research on infants in ECE are clearly no less relevant today than they were in the 1990s. The difference appears to be that while more is now known about what constitutes quality, about what this 'looks like' for infants in ECE, and about the consequences for society if these are ignored, little has changed concerning implementation of policies that support high quality (Dalli, 2017). We assert that this is due to a lack of advocacy for infants' rights at a policy level rather than in the commitment of ECEC teachers who work with infants. Recently, the OECD (2015) declared that access to quality ECE services for infants is now an urgent global priority and a societal imperative. A rights agenda is possibly even more important today than ever before given the neoliberal climate that prevails.

Looking to the future, there is much to be gained by persisting with a sociocultural advocacy agenda for infants. This national and international agenda would shift the emphasis away from an acceptance that a higher level of quality depends on parents' ability to pay for it, towards a government commitment to fund better-quality ECE. Instead of locating infants as a burden or a commodity, or suggesting that ECE services are a less positive alternative that ought to be avoided (O'Neill, 2016), a sociocultural approach engages communities collectively to act in the best interests of infants. With that approach, communities would pay heed to what is now widely known to constitute high-quality ECE and urge governments to respond with appropriate policies and funding. There is good evidence to suggest that such initiatives are of benefit not only to infants and their families but also to wider society—both now and in the future. Those who are cared for now will be those who care for our world when we are no longer able to do so.

## References

Barraclough, S. J. (1994). *Parent choice and childcare quality: A New Zealand study*. Unpublished MEd research report, University of Otago.

Barraclough, S. J., & Smith, A. B. (1996). Do parents choose and value quality childcare in New Zealand? *International Journal of Early Years Education*, 4(1), 5–26.

Dalli, C. (2017). Tensions and challenges in professional practice with under-threes: A New Zealand reflection on early childhood professionalism as a systemic phenomenon. In E. J. White & C. Dalli (Eds.), *Under-three year olds in policy and practice*. Dordrecht. The Netherlands: Springer.

Dalli, C., Rockel, J., Duhn, I., Craw, J., with Doyle, K. (2011). *What's special about teaching and learning in the first years? Summary report*. Wellington: Teaching & Learning Research Initiative.

Dalli, C., & White, E. J. (2016). Group-based early education and care for under-2-year olds: Quality debates, pedagogy and lived experience. In A. Farrell, S. L. Kagan, & E. K. M. Tisdall (Eds.), *The Sage handbook of early childhood research* (pp. 36–54). London, UK: Sage.

Dalli, C., White, E. J., Rockel, J., Duhn, I., Buchanan, E., Davidson, S., et al. (2011). *Quality early childhood education for under-two-year-olds: What should it look like? A literature review*. Report to Ministry of Education, Wellington. Retrieved from http://www.educationcounts.govt.nz/publications/ECE/Quality ECE_for under-two-year-olds.

Harrison, L., & Sumsion, J. (2014). *Lived spaces of infant-toddler education and care: Exploring diverse perspectives on theory, research, practice and policy*. Dordrecht, The Netherlands: Springer.

Li, L., Quinones, G., & Ridgway, A. (Eds.) (in press). *Studying babies and toddlers: Relationships in cultural contexts*. Dordrecht, The Netherlands: Springer.

Johansson, E. (2011). Introduction: Giving words to children's voices in research, In E. Johansson & E. J. White (Eds.), *Educational research with our youngest: Voices of infants and toddlers*. (pp. 1–6). Sydney, NSW: Springer.

Johansson, E., & White, E. J. (Eds.). (2011). *Educational research with our youngest: Voices of infants and toddlers*. Dordrecht, The Netherlands: Springer.

Mathers, S., Eisenstadt, N., Sylva, K., Soukakou, E., & Ereky-Severs, K. (2014). *Sound foundations: A review of the research evidence on quality education and care for children under three: Implications for policy and practice*. Oxford, UK: University of Oxford and The Sutton Trust.

Ministry of Education. (1996). *Te whāriki: Early childhood curriculum*. Wellington: Learning Media.

Moss, P. (2008). Beyond quality in early childhood education and care: Languages of evaluation. *New Zealand Journal of Teachers' Work, 5*(1), 3–12.

OECD. (2015). PF3: Enrolment in childcare and preschool. *OECD family database*. Retrieved from https://www.oecd.org/els/soc/PF3_2_Enrolment_childcare_preschool.pdf.

O'Neill, K. (2016). *Behind the headlines: Early childhood education and care: A literature review*. Auckland: Brainwave Trust Aotearoa.

Rayna, S. (2010). Research and ECEC for children under three in France: A brief review. *International Journal of Early Childhood, 42*(2), 117–130.

Ridgeway, A., Liang, L., & Quinones, G. (2016) Visual narrative methodology in educational research with babies: Triadic play in babies' rooms [video]. *Video Journal of Education and Pedagogy*. Retrieved from http://videoeducationjournal.springeropen.com/articles/10.1186/s40990-016-0005-0.

Rogoff, B. (2003). *The cultural nature of human development*. New York, NY: Oxford University Press.

Smith, A. B. (1996a). Is quality a subjective or objective matter? In A. B Smith & N. J. Taylor (Eds.), *Assessing and improving quality in early childhood centres*. Dunedin: Children's Issues Centre, University of Otago.

Smith, A. B. (1996b). *The quality of childcare centres for infants in New Zealand*. State-of-the-art monograph, No. 4. Palmerston North: New Zealand Association for Research in Education.

Smith, A. B. (1999). Quality childcare and joint attention. *International Journal of Early Years Education, 7*(1), 85–98.

Smith, A. B. (2015). Early childhood education in New Zealand: Progress and challenges in achieving children's rights. In A. B. Smith (Ed.), *Enhancing children's rights: Connecting research, policy and practice* (pp. 80–94). Basingstoke, UK: Palgrave Macmillan.

Smith, A. B., & Barraclough, S. J. (1997). Quality childcare: Do parents choose it? *Early Childhood Folio, 3*, 19–22.

Smith, A. B., & Barraclough, S. J. (1999). Young children's conflicts and teachers' perspectives on them. *New Zealand Journal of Educational Studies, 34*, 1–2.

Smith, A. B., Barraclough, S., & Sutcliffe, R. (1996). *Young children's conflicts and teachers' perspectives on them: Research report to the Ministry of Education*. Dunedin: Children's Issues Centre, University of Otago.

Stephen, C., Dunlop, A. W. & Trevarthen, C. (2003). *Meeting the needs of children from birth to three: Research evidence and implications for out-of-home provision.* Insight 6. Edinburgh, UK: Scottish Executive Education Department.

Sylva, K., Melhuish, E., Sammons, P., Siraj-Blatchford, I., Taggart, B., & Elliot, K. (2003). *The Effective Provision of Pre-School Education (EPPE) project: Findings from the pre-school period.* London, UK: EPPE Office, Institute of Education, University of London.

White, E. J. (2016a). *Introducing dialogic pedagogy: Provocations for the early years.* London, UK: Routledge.

White, E. J. (2016b). More than meets the 'I': A polyphonic approach to dialogic meaning-making [video]. *Video Journal of Education and Pedagogy.* Retrieved from http://videoeducationjournal.springeropen.com/articles/10.1186/s40990-016-0002-3.

White, E. J., & Dalli, C. (Eds.). (2017). *Under three-year-olds in policy and practice.* Dordrecht, The Netherlands: Springer.

White, E. J. & Mika, C. (2013). Coming of age? Infants and toddlers in curriculum. In J. Nuttall (Ed.), *Weaving Te Whāriki* (2nd ed., pp. 93–115). Wellington: NZCER Press.

White, E. J., Peter, M., & Ranger, G. (in press). Two-year-olds in ECE: A policy issue for New Zealand? *Early Childhood Folio.*

White, E. J., & Redder, B. (2015). Proximity with under two-year-olds in early childhood education: A silent pedagogical encounter. *Early Education and Care.* doi: 10.1080/03004430.2015.1028386.

Whitebook, M., Howes, C., & Phillips, D. (1989). *Who cares? Child care teachers and the quality of care in America.* Final Report National Child Care Staffing Study. Oakland, CA: Child Care Employee Project.

# Chapter 4 Children's participation in Finnish early childhood education

Janniina Vlasov, Leena Turja, Anne Valpas and Eeva Hujala

*Introduction*

Contemporary childhood studies, the United Nations Convention on the Rights of the Child (1989) and international recommendations have guided the policies and practices of early childhood education and care (ECEC) around the world by viewing children as actively participating subjects in their own lives (Taylor & Smith, 2015). In line with current trends, Finnish ECEC has undergone significant changes at both the administrative and the policy levels, and there are ongoing reforms to ECEC legislation and the National Curriculum Guidelines (STAKES, 2005). Today, ECEC in Finland is legislatively seen as the right of a child.

After the administration of ECEC was shifted from the Ministry of Social Affairs and Health to the Ministry of Education and Culture in 2013, early childhood education was officially acknowledged and considered as the first phase of a lifelong learning path. With this administrative shift the societal task of childcare changed from a task related to social welfare and labour force policy to one emphasising children's right to early education and learning. The shift highlights children's ownership of their own lifelong learning and their role as active and equal members of society. This chapter aims to describe the current situation of the Finnish ECEC system by focusing on children's participation in early education and describing how it has changed from the point of view of educators. We start by framing the general context of Finnish ECEC. After laying down the societal premises, we describe how children's participation is implemented in Finnish ECEC and how it has developed. Finally, we introduce a research-based model that considers children's participation.

## *Framing the context of Finnish early childhood education and care*

Finnish ECEC can be seen to follow the Nordic idea of an institutionalised and universal childcare system which is guided by legislation and national policies (Karila, 2012). Finnish ECEC is intricately connected to the societal task of advancing children's equality and equity (Alila, 2013): irrespective of the socioeconomic status of parents, all children are entitled to access to universal childcare either full or part time. As research has shown, universal ECEC has an important role in levelling out socioeconomic differences between groups in long-term learning outcomes (Sylva, Melhuish, Sammons, Siraj-Blatchford, & Taggart, 2010) and preventing social exclusion (Kajanoja, 1999), both of which have been considered important in the Finnish ECEC system.

As in many other countries, ECEC in Finland covers the age range of birth to 8 years. What makes the system exceptional is that, in addition to the variety of ECEC programmes, the pre-primary year as well as the first and second years in primary school are seen as being part of early childhood education. The pedagogy and didactics for ECEC and the first years in school aim to support children's learning through play and enhance learning-to-learn skills instead of focusing on academic outcomes. The overall objectives of Finnish educational policies support children's growth as human beings and enhance the competencies required for acting as members of a democratic society and supporting the ideals of sustainability (Halinen, Harmanen, & Mattila, 2015).

Instead of strict learning goals, Finnish ECEC aims to promote the age- and developmentally appropriate growth, health and wellbeing of children, and to support the prerequisites for lifelong learning (Finnish National Board of Education, 2016). The focus of the Finnish national curricula at all levels of education is to support children's growth and development as individuals and citizens of Finnish society. In the renewed core curricula (ECEC, pre-primary, primary education) the broad objectives for learning are described as areas of competence. In ECEC these interconnected areas are (1) thinking skills and learning to learn, (2) cultural competence, interaction and expression, (3) managing daily life, taking care of oneself and others, (4) multi-literacy, (5) ICT-competence, (6) participation, influence and building a sustainable future.

The competencies for learning are required in order to prepare children to meet the demands of a rapidly changing society. Learning competencies should be taken into account in the everyday pedagogical practices with children in a developmentally appropriate way: the younger the child, the more help they need from the adults around them. The aim of varied pedagogically planned and implemented activities and shared experiences with educators and peers is to promote the development of knowledge, skills, values and attitudes of children. Children are gently supported to take responsibility for their own actions, their relationship with others and the surrounding environment (Finnish National Board of Education, 2016). This forms the basis for democratic and participatory pedagogy. The competencies for learning highlight the principles of discovery learning, which aim to enhance children's activity, initiative, responsibility, influence and choice (Lipponen, 2011).

### *Integrated education and care*

The pedagogical premises of Finnish ECEC reflect the ideals of a learning community that fosters warm interaction, a wide range of working methods and children's right to joy in learning through play. The roots of the Finnish ECEC system derive from Friedrich Fröebel's kindergarten pedagogy, which still influences professional practice, even if the theoretical basis for early education is now broader. Policies guiding Finnish ECEC are based on socio-constructivist and contextual theoretical orientations to understanding children's development (Hujala, 1996), in which children are viewed as active and competent actors in their own lives. Learning is seen as taking place in constant interaction and dialogue with the environment.

The Finnish ECEC model is based on the holistic approach, which comprises education, teaching and care in an integrated model, widely known as 'educare' (Smith, 1996). In her many publications (Smith, 1987, 1992; Smith & Swain, 1988) Anne Smith was a pioneer in theorising and defining educare as a new concept in early childhood education. Before the adoption of the construct of educare, education and care were seen as quite separate. Care was seen as custodial physical care provided mainly for children under 3 years old. Education was defined as planned activities designed for older children to enhance their learning. Anne Smith (1996) emphasised that there is no need to distinguish education and care. She suggested (1996, p. 91) that "small children do not easily learn in environments where their physical and emotional wellbeing is not nurtured". Smith examined early childhood education and children's learning from the point of view of the social and cultural context and based her theoretical considerations on a Vygotskian sociocultural paradigm. Finnish early childhood education—both research and practice—has benefited from the theoretical foundations of her educare thinking (Hujala, Puroila, Parrila-Haapakoski, & Nivala, 1998).

Anne Smith was one of the pioneers of bringing the child's voice into an understanding of pedagogy in early childhood education. She emphasised that children do not passively absorb the strategies of the adult; instead, children have an active role in constructing their own unique understanding within the sociocultural context (Smith, 1996, 2002). Teaching with a focus on children's participation is seen as a process of sharing meaning and understanding. Children's participation in the ECEC context has been the focus of the research of many scholars around the world, including some recent Finnish researchers (Kangas, 2016; Roos, 2015; Virkki, 2015).

The roots of children's participation are to be found in the United Nations Convention on the Rights of the Child (1989), which states that every child has a right to be heard on matters that affect their lives and to freely express their thoughts. These commitments have guided the work of researchers and practitioners in all societal fields and, together with increasing scientific and practical knowledge, have put pressure on the government to develop Finnish legislation to enhance children's participation. This is evident in the revised Act on Early Childhood Education and Care (36/1973; 2015), in which children's right to participation has finally been given a legal status, ensuring that all children have the possibility of participating in matters concerning them. The law now explicitly determines that children and their parents or custodians should be given an opportunity to participate in and influence the planning and evaluation processes in ECEC on a regular basis.

## *Children's participation in Finnish ECEC*

Turja (2006, 2016) has studied changes in children's participation and has developed a model of how it works in the Finnish ECEC context by collecting narratives from educators attending in-service training days around the country during the last 10 years. Analysis of the narratives reveals that both the understanding of the nature of children's participation, as well as the practices to enhance it, have clearly changed over the last decade. There have been changes both in the planning of pedagogical practices and in the way educators are positioning themselves in relation to the children. In the narratives collected during the first years of the study, children usually had to take the initiative themselves if they wanted to contribute to the ongoing activities and existing schedules, routines and environments planned by the staff while, for the most part, the adults acted as gatekeepers of children's participation by accepting or denying their suggestions. By contrast, in the narratives collected recently, it is increasingly common for staff to invite the children to plan together with the adults. Typically, children are more likely to be allowed to contribute to such activities and in environments that are 'less scripted', such as art, music and gym activities, nature visits in the neighbourhood, free playtime and outdoor time. However, adults still quite tightly control daily routines and schedules.

In the more advanced participatory practices, the educators take the topics that interest the children as main themes to guide the activities and take care that the objectives of various subject areas and developmental domains are embedded in the thematic activities. Children have the opportunity to participate in the whole process—from planning and implementation, to evaluating activities and the environmental arrangements—as much as possible, depending on, for example, their age and experience. The educators may also collect all the ideas of the children in the class to be voted on, or implemented in turn. The sphere of influence of children's participation varies to encompass their personal issues and issues in the classroom or in the whole centre; in some cases their action may be influential and visible even in the wider community. In addition, the duration of children's participatory action can vary from single-activity sessions to whole-day programmes, and even to projects over several weeks. Sometimes the duration of action is relatively short, but it has long-lasting effects as children are involved in designing their play and learning areas, or take part in negotiating the rules for the group, or have a say in the acquisition of new toys and other materials.

The most advanced practitioners' narratives are even indicating a 'turn' in pedagogical planning. Instead of planning activities by themselves, educators have said that they have now started to plan how the children can plan these activities. They schedule time for joint discussions and negotiations with the children about planning and decision making in the group. Children's empowerment is also seen in the ways the educators position themselves during the ongoing pedagogical activities. This is in line with Hart's (1992) ladder model of children's participation, in which the different rungs of the ladder represent different levels in the power balance between adults and children. In this model, the top rung of the ladder corresponds to pedagogical practices that allow children to have ideas, set up a project and invite the adults to join in to carry it out. In other words, the adults are not in charge, nor are they helpers for children's own projects; rather, they are working side by side with the children.

The dimensions of participation in the model Turja (2016) has developed are: the *empowerment of children*, where the adult–child power balance is central; the *sphere of children's participation* extending beyond their own issues to the wider community; and the *time frame of participation*, referring both to the duration of an activity or project and the duration of its effects, as highlighted above. Turja argues that the fundamental prerequisites for children's participation have to do with *trust, communication, knowledge* and *material resources*. Both the children and the adults need to have trust in other people as well as in themselves as actors in order to have courage to participate in a group. Educators have to trust both children's capabilities and their own management. Trust enables educators to act with confidence in situations that are open and less controlled or pre-planned by adults, and conducted together with children. The educators need to communicate in ways that enable every child to feel understood as well as enable each child to understand as well as remember. Such functional communication is a foundation for mutual trust and makes information on matters that are important in the children's life accessible. This knowledge determines their opportunities to develop and present relevant suggestions and ideas, and to initiate activities. Access to knowledge is also crucial in Hart's (1992) model. Access to materials and places means that children can explore various possibilities and put their ideas into practice.

Finally, according to the staff narratives, successful participation experiences have produced various positive *emotional states*, both for children and for adults, and for individuals as well as groups. Examples of positive emotional states are increased feelings of trust and self-confidence. Listening to the children's viewpoints and giving them room to take the pre-planned activities in new directions have also offered a mirror for the educators to see their own pedagogical thinking and practices. This has led to critical reflections as a part of their professional development.

However, the changes in the pedagogical work of Finnish educators are not without problems. A recent study (Kangas, 2016) has demonstrated that children's initiatives and participation are considered important by Finnish early educators, but that structural and institutional rules seem to restrict the implementation of a participatory pedagogy, including children's possibilities for taking part in the pedagogical decision-making processes. Virkki (2015) has studied children's agency and participation in the everyday activities in ECEC, from both the child's and the adult's perspectives. The results suggest a discrepancy between the rhetoric and implementation of a participatory pedagogy in terms of how educators and children view children's possibilities and ways of participating. Early educators did not always seem to recognise the effects that children's interaction with their peers and their initiatives had on the pedagogical activities. The Finnish study on ECEC quality across the country confirms these findings: it found that children's participation in daily activities does not occur at the expected level or as hoped (Hujala, Fonsén, & Elo, 2012). Nonetheless, as studies by Turja (2016, 2006) confirm, Finnish ECEC is on the right track in acknowledging children's right to participate, and that this needs to be taken into account in planning, implementing and evaluating pedagogical practices.

## Conclusion

The move towards children's participation in ECEC practices is influenced by professional development on the local level, but it is also strongly dependent on contextual factors in a given society. Finland ratified the UN Convention on the Rights of the Child in 1991, which has in turn favourably affected legislative reforms and state-level curriculum guidance. The possibilities for children's participation are strongly grounded in the values of Finnish society, such as the principles of democracy and equality, as well as in contemporary understanding of children's learning and development.

In addition to societal values and policy reforms, a pedagogy that supports children's participation has to begin with a transformation of the educators' attitudes, the development of pedagogical practices and the eventual consolidation of new practices (e.g. Shier, 2001). It is important that educators develop a shared and mutual understanding about what children's participation in everyday practices and pedagogy means and why it is important. The majority of Finnish educators have a strong desire for participatory pedagogy, but the practices have remained largely adult centred (e.g. Kangas, 2016).

The model developed by Turja (together with ECEC staff) can help educators to outline the different factors that influence children's participation in ECEC. We acknowledge that the shift towards increasing children's participation calls for support through structural variables, such as favourable adult:child ratios and small group size, but also the maintenance of the pedagogical autonomy of the teachers. It is equally important to ensure the flexible integration of children's ideas into the programme that there are no pressures of formal assessment of the children's learning outcomes. This also means it is important to gain parents' support for, and understanding of the value of, children's participation, together with parents' own participation in early childhood educational processes. Although children's and parents' right to participate and influence the ECEC programmes is now incorporated in legislation and the guiding policy documents, it will require conscious and systematic work from the ECEC staff to involve both children and their parents in the planning and evaluation processes of the programmes. More research is needed to guide this development work.

## *References*

Alila, K. (2013). *Varhaiskasvatuksen laadun ohjaus ja ohjauksen laatu: Laatupuhe varhaiskasvatuksen valtionhallinnon asiakirjoissa 1972–2012.* [Guiding quality assurance of early childhood education and quality of that guidance: Discourses of quality in guiding national documents in 1972–2012]. Acta Universitatis Tamperensis 1824. Tampere, Finland: Tampere University Press.

Finnish National Board of Education. (2016). *National core curriculum on early childhood education and care orders and guidelines.* Helsinki, Finland

Halinen, I., Harmanen, M., & Mattila, P. (2015). Making sense of complexity of the world today: Why Finland is introducing multiliteracy in teaching and learning. In V. Bozsik (Ed.), *Improving literacy skills across learning* (pp. 136–153). CIDREE Yearbook 2015. Budapest, Hungary: HIERD. Retrieved from http://www.oph.fi/download/173262_cidree_yb_2015_halinen_harmanen_mattila.pdf

Hart, R. A. (1992). *Children's participation: From tokenism to citizenship.* Florence, Italy: UNICEF.

Hujala, E. (1996). Varhaiskasvatuksen teoreettisen kehyksen rakentuminen [Constructing the theoretical frame for early childhood education]. *Kasvatus, 27*(5), 489–500.

Hujala, E., Fonsén, E., & Elo, J. (2012). Evaluating the quality of the child care in Finland. *Early Child Development and Care, 182*(3–4), 299–314.

Hujala, E., Puroila, A.-M., Parrila-Haapakoski, S., & Nivala, V. (1998). *Päivähoidosta varhaiskasvatukseen* [From daycare service to early childhood education]. Jyväskylä: Varhaiskasvatus 90.

Kajanoja, J. (1999). *Lasten päivähoito investointina* [Children's day care as an investigation]. Tutkimuksia 50. Helsinki, Finland: Valtion taloudellinen tutkimuskeskus.

Kangas, J. (2016). *Enhancing children's participation in early childhood education with participatory pedagogy.* Helsinki, Finland: Faculty of Behavioural Sciences, Department of Teacher Education, University of Helsinki.

Karila, K. (2012). A Nordic perspective on early childhood education and care policy. *European Journal of Education, 47*(4), 584–595.

Lipponen, L. (2011). Tutkiva oppiminen varhaispedagogiikassa [Explorative learning in ECE pedagogy]. In E. Hujala & L. Turja (Eds.), *Varhaiskasvatuksen käsikirja* [The handbook of early childhood education] (pp. 31–38). Jyväskylä, Finland: PS-kustannus.

Roos, P. (2015). *Lasten kerrontaa päiväkotiarjesta* [Children's narration of the daily life in a child care centre]. Tampere, Finland: Juvenes Print.

Shier, H. (2001). Pathways to participation: Openings, opportunities and obligations: A new model for enhancing children's participation in decision-making, in line with Article 12.1 of the United Nations Convention on the Rights of the Child. *Children and Society, 15*(2), 107-117.

Smith, A. B. (1987). Recent developments in early childhood 'educare' in New Zealand. *International Journal of Early Childhood, 19*(2), 33–43.

Smith, A. (1992). Early childhood educare: Seeking a theoretical framework in Vygotsky's work. *International Journal of Early Years Learning, 1*(1), 47–61.

Smith, A. B. (1996). Early childhood educare: Quality programmes which care and educate. In E. Hujala (Ed.), *Childhood education: International perspectives* (pp. 89–103). Oulu, Finland: University of Oulu & Finland Association for Childhood Education International.

Smith, A. B. (2002). Supporting participatory rights: Contributions from sociocultural theory. *International Journal of Children's Rights, 10*(1), 73–88.

Smith, A. B., & Swain, D. A. (1988). *Child care in New Zealand: People, programmes, politics*. Wellington: Allen & Unwin / Port Nicholson Press.

STAKES. (2005). *National curriculum guidelines on early childhood and care in Finland*. Helsinki, Finland: Author. Retrieved from http://www.julkari.fi/bitstream/handle/10024/75535/267671cb-0ec0-4039-b97b-7ac6ce6b9c10.pdf?sequence=1

Sylva, K., Melhuish, E., Sammons, P., Siraj Blatchford, I., & Taggart, B. (Eds.). (2010). *Early childhood matters: Evidence from the Effective Preschool and Primary Education project*. Oxford, UK: Routledge.

Taylor, N., & Smith, A. B. (2015). Thinking about children: How does it influence policy and practice? In J. Wyn & H. Cahill (Eds.), *Handbook of children and youth studies* (pp. 49–62). Singapore: Springer.

Turja, L. (2006, August). *"This opened my eyes": Teachers' narratives about children's participation in and contribution to the practice of ECE*. Paper presented at EECERA Conference: Democracy and Culture in Early Childhood Education, University of Reykjavik, Reykjavik, Iceland.

Turja, L. (2016). Lasten osallisuus varhaiskasvatuksessa [Children's participation in early childhood education]. In E. Hujala & L. Turja (Eds.), *Varhaiskasvatuksen käsikirja* [The handbook of early childhood education] (3rd ed., pp. 41–54). Jyväskylä, Finland: PS-kustannus.

Virkki, P. (2015). *Varhaiskasvatus toimijuuden ja osallisuuden edistäjänä* [ECE as a promoter of agency and participation]. Dissertations in education, humanities and theology 66. Joensuu: University of Eastern Finland.

# Chapter 5  Children's rights in Aotearoa New Zealand

Nicola Taylor and Sarah Te One

### *Introduction*

The New Zealand Government ratified the United Nations Convention on the Rights of the Child (UNCRC) in 1993, just 2 years before the establishment of the Children's Issues Centre (CIC) at the University of Otago, with Anne Smith as its foundation director. Smith had already established herself as a leading researcher and advocate in the early childhood field, and the CIC provided the platform for an expansion of research and advocacy into other key aspects of children's rights, development and wellbeing. This chapter briefly outlines the genesis of advocacy for children's rights internationally and then draws on New Zealand's UNCRC reporting process, including the various periodic and alternative reports and concluding observations from 1997 to 2016, to highlight significant steps taken in New Zealand (including by the CIC under Anne Smith's leadership) to abolish the physical punishment of children (Article 19) and to promote the participation rights of children (Article 12), including in quality early childhood education (Article 29) .

## *The genesis of the UNCRC*

At the end of World War I Eglantyne Jebb, a children's activist, formed the Save the Children International Union out of concern for the horror of war inflicted on children (Smith, 2016). In 1923 this Union drafted a half-page declaration that was adopted by the Fifth Assembly of the League of Nations and renamed the *Geneva Declaration of the Rights of the Child* (1924). Members of the League of Nations were invited to follow its principles based on the premise that "mankind owes to the child the best it has to give". In 1959 the United Nations (UN) expanded on the Geneva Declaration by adopting the three-page *Declaration of the Rights of the Child*, which emphasised children's material needs; it was aspirational and not legally binding.

Two decades later, in 1978, in anticipation of the 1979 International Year of the Child, Poland proposed the adoption of a children's rights convention. The Polish government submitted a draft text with 10 articles and implementing provisions to the UN Commission on Human Rights, which consulted with governments, non-government organisations (NGOs) and various UN bodies and established a working group. The feedback generated through these processes enabled Poland to produce a new draft with 20 articles. Over the next decade the working group engaged in lengthy debate and worked with numerous groups—though not with children—to reshape the Polish text into its current form. The UNCRC was adopted by the UN General Assembly on 20 November 1989, 30 years to the day after the adoption of the *UN Declaration on the Rights of the Child*.

The UNCRC, a landmark for the children's rights movement, is one of the six core international conventions and covenants aimed at promoting and protecting human rights. Its significance lies in the fact that it is the first international instrument bringing together the ratifying countries' obligations with respect to the protection, provision and participation rights of children under the age of 18 years. The UNCRC provides an internationally agreed framework of civil, political, cultural, social, economic and humanitarian standards against which legislation, policies and practices can be measured and their ongoing compliance monitored. While acknowledging children as rights holders, it also firmly recognises the interdependence of children, parents and society.

The UNCRC had the fastest ratification process of any UN human rights treaty. By 1990 there were sufficient ratifications to put it into force, and it has now been ratified by all but two countries: the USA (which is a signatory) and South Sudan. Ratification means that a government has agreed to be bound by international law to adopt appropriate measures to achieve the minimum standards set out in the UNCRC and to allocate the maximum amount of available resources in order to ensure its implementation.

The New Zealand government became a signatory to the UNCRC in 1990 and formally ratified it in 1993. Three reservations were entered (which remain in place today) relating to: the non-provision of benefits to children unlawfully in the country (Article 28); the adequacy of measures to protect children in employment (Article 32); and the mixing of juvenile and adult prisoners (Article 37). Two of the three optional protocols to the UNCRC have been ratified by New Zealand: the Involvement of Children in Armed Conflict (ratified in 2001); and the Sale of Children, Child Prostitution and Child Pornography (ratified in 2011). However, the most recent optional protocol establishing a complaints procedure has been neither signed nor ratified by New Zealand.

## *The UNCRC reporting process*

Countries that have ratified the UNCRC, called 'States Parties' by the United Nations, are required to report to the UN Committee on the Rights of the Child (a body of 18 experts elected by the States Parties, which meets in Geneva) on their progress in implementing and complying with the Convention 2 years after ratification and every 5 years thereafter (Article 44). At the time of writing New Zealand has recently completed its fifth periodic reporting cycle, with previous government reports having been submitted by the Ministries of Youth Affairs (1995, 2000), Youth Development (2008, combined third and fourth periodic reports) and Social Development (2015). Given the robust role for NGOs within the UN reporting processes, alternative reports have also been submitted setting out the issues facing New Zealand children during each phase by Action for Children and Youth Aotearoa (ACYA, 1996, 2003, 2010, 2015). The UN Committee's concluding observations on New Zealand's compliance with the UNCRC and recommendations for government action were published in 1997, 2003 and 2011, with the most recent document provided in October 2016 following completion of the fifth periodic reporting cycle.

## *The abolition of physical punishment*

> Corporal punishment is a direct assault on the human dignity of the child and a direct invasion of the child's physical integrity. (Newell, 2011, p. 7)

Physical punishment was widely accepted as a family discipline strategy in New Zealand homes and schools. A large-scale survey in 1981 found that 92 percent of men and 86 percent of women endorsed physical punishment in certain circumstances (Ritchie & Ritchie, 1981). Until 2007, when a parent (or a person in the place of a parent) was prosecuted for assault on a child, parents could invoke the defence in section 59 of the Crimes Act 1961 to avoid conviction by claiming that the force they used (i) was reasonable in the circumstances, and (ii) was for the purpose of correcting the child's behaviour. The section 59 defence led to many acquittals (especially by juries) for serious assaults on children (Taylor, Wood, & Smith, 2011). Similar defences used to exist to protect the physical punishment meted out to wives, servants, sailors and apprentices. While such violence against adults had subsequently been banned, this did not extend to children. Corporal punishment was prohibited in New Zealand schools in 1990, but its use within the home remained commonplace.

Article 19 of the UNCRC does not specifically mention physical punishment, but it does state that children should be protected from all forms of physical or mental violence and notes the importance of protective measures to support children and their parents/carers. In 2006 the UN Committee on the Rights of the Child, in "General Comment No. 8", clearly stated that physical punishment of children is a human rights infringement and that states are obligated to eliminate it. The Committee defined corporal or physical punishment as "any punishment in which physical force is used and intended to cause some degree of pain or discomfort, however light" (para. 11). "General Comment No. 13" (2011) on Article 19 (freedom from all forms of violence) describes the right of the child to protection from corporal punishment and other cruel or degrading forms of punishment. Article 3 (the child's best interests) cannot be used to justify practices that conflict with a child's human dignity and right to physical integrity.

When examining New Zealand's initial (1995) and second (2000) periodic reports to the UN, the UN Committee (1997, 2003) took the opportunity to comment on section 59. It urged the prohibition of corporal punishment in the home and the promotion of positive, non-violent child-rearing through parental education and public awareness campaigns. These recommendations were made to more than 130 states.

In New Zealand, Anne Smith, as director of the CIC, took the UN Committee's urgings seriously. In 2005 the CIC published a review of the international research evidence on the *discipline and guidance of children* (Smith, Gollop, Taylor, & Marshall, 2005). True to the UNCRC commitment to children's participation rights, the CIC included the perspectives of children in its advocacy to ban the use of physical punishment (Smith, 2013, 2015a, 2016). Their perspectives had been gathered when CIC researchers asked New Zealand children about parental disciplinary practices (Dobbs, Smith, & Taylor, 2006). Children's views on physical punishment, a disciplinary method they had experienced a lot, were subsequently given widespread media coverage. They were also cited in the CIC (2006) submission to the Select Committee considering a Bill in Parliament in 2005 that sought to repeal section 59. The Private Member's Bill triggered public debate that polarised the nation. Many people were concerned that any change to the law would risk the criminalisation of loving parents or be impossible to enforce. Others said that physically punishing children did no harm. Some commented that what was needed was greater clarity in the law about how children could be smacked safely (e.g. no use of implements, no hits to their head and neck). Section 59 of the Crimes Act 1961 was amended by the Crimes (Substituted Section 59) Amendment Act 2007, and took effect from 21 June 2007. Four exceptions allow the use of reasonable force (but not for the purpose of correction) and reaffirm police discretion.

New Zealand thus became the first English-speaking country to prohibit all physical punishment of children, and this was warmly welcomed by the UN Committee (2011, para 28). As at October 2016, 49 other countries afford similar protection to children.

## Early childhood care and education and participation rights

> What happens to young children matters a lot, and if children don't have access to top quality early childhood education during the early years, it is a missed opportunity to have a positive impact on their lifelong learning. (A. Smith, personal communication, 21 July 2010)

The UNCRC does not specifically mention early childhood care and education (ECCE) rights, but in New Zealand it is widely agreed that Article 29—articulating children's rights to reach their potential—extends to the early childhood sector. *General Comment No. 7* (2005) on early childhood foregrounded the important role ECCE services play for children and their families. The *Comment* explicitly links early education to children's development (2005, para 28) and notes that

> the growing body of theory and research … confirms that young children are best understood as social actors whose survival, wellbeing and development is dependent on and built around close relationships. (2005, para 8)

Children's right to access high-quality ECCE has been highlighted in ACYA's alternative reports (1996, 2003, 2010, 2015) to the UN Committee on the Rights of the Child. In 2011, in response to the 2010 report, the UN Committee made the following recommendation:

> Ensure that all children have access to high quality early childhood education and care that, at a minimum, is free for socially disadvantaged families and children. (*Concluding Recommendations*, 2011, para 44 (a))

In New Zealand, active campaigning for young children's rights to quality ECCE dates back to the 1970s (e.g. see Smith, 1980, 1993). In the early 1980s feminist advocacy for women's rights to equal opportunity (and pay) included advocacy for the provision of high-quality childcare. An early evaluative study of infant child care provision (Smith, 1996) argued for the adoption of internationally recognised quality measures: small group size, qualified teachers, and high teacher:child ratios. An important finding was that ECCE services of high quality built children's resilience and supported their long-term wellbeing across a range of domains. The opposite was found to be true:

ECCE services that did not meet quality standards had the potential to damage children.

Policy development in ECCE in the last two decades has had mixed impacts (Te One, 2010). Gains made under a Labour-led coalition government during the 2000s to promote quality improvements were rapidly dismantled by the National-led government (2009 to the present day). Recent government policy has prioritised 'participation' over quality measures such as qualified staff (Ritchie, Harvey, Kayes, & Smith, 2014). Several Education Review Office reports (2012, 2013, 2015) and a recent Advisory Group report (Ministry of Education, 2015) have recommended that professional development be funded for teachers to enhance their capacity to deliver the national early childhood education curriculum, *Te Whāriki*. However, teachers have been denied this support. Currently, the national average of staff who are qualified teachers sits below 75 percent (Education Counts, 2014). This is of serious concern, particularly in the absence of universally available in-service support for professional learning and development (ACYA, 2015) and the overwhelming evidence that in-depth teacher education is one of the most important elements of high-quality ECCE.

During her time at the CIC, Anne Smith worked to link her interest in the UNCRC with debates on quality ECCE. This interest was seminal to an emerging children's rights discourse in the early childhood sector and was certainly influential in the debates on quality ECCE. Smith's (2015b) research provided examples of how children's participation rights (Article 12) complemented their rights to development and learning (Article 29). She said that protecting children included protecting their participation rights in quality early childhood education. Providing young children with opportunities to participate and make choices acknowledges them as citizens and as experts in relation to their own lives.

Smith argued that participation in ECCE services, while important, should not be at the expense of quality provision. The long-standing aspirations of many in the sector to universally accessible and free ECCE of high quality have become clouded in the present political climate. An increase in private sector provision has coincided with greater emphasis on enrolments and diminished attention to high-quality ECCE. Terms like 'priority learners' and 'vulnerable children' have been introduced alongside policies that target ECCE spending. Smith courageously challenged the focus on vulnerability, arguing that targeted provision at the expense of universal provision was short sighted. At the same time, she noted that workforce policy changes such as reducing the requirement for qualified staff, and cuts to New Zealand-based research like the Early Childhood Education Centres of Innovation programme, are likely to have detrimental consequences for all children and families (Smith, 2012). The quality of ECCE remains a vital and enduring issue.

## Conclusion

> The UNCRC provides a holistic, unifying vision of children's rights and childhood, and provides child advocates, professionals working with children, and policy-makers, with a direction and moral imperative for improving policies and practices for children. (Smith, 2016, p. 155)

In her final book, Anne Smith (2016) highlighted the importance of championing children's rights in sociocultural contexts. She had a profound impact on shifting people's understanding of children to viewing them as people/citizens in their own right, entitled to be treated with respect and to have their perspectives taken seriously. Her work also reminds us that it is through positive social relationships with other people (especially family members and those working closely with children) in supportive environments that children acquire knowledge and the opportunity for their rights, development, agency and wellbeing to thrive. Anne's fearless child-centred, evidence-based advocacy to ban the physical punishment of children and to demand high-quality ECCE was grounded in her commitment to the fundamental rights and dignity of children. This wisdom should not be forgotten.

## References

ACYA (Action for Children and Youth Aotearoa). (1996). *Action for children Aotearoa*. Auckland: Author.

ACYA (Action for Children and Youth Aotearoa). (2003). *Children and youth in Aotearoa 2003*. Auckland: Author.

ACYA (Action for Children and Youth Aotearoa). (2010). *Children and youth in Aotearoa 2010*. Auckland: Author.

ACYA (Action for Children and Youth Aotearoa). (2015). *UNCRC alternative report*. Auckland: Author.

CIC (Children's Issues Centre). (2006). *Submission to the Justice and Electoral Select Committee of the New Zealand Parliament*. Dunedin: University of Otago.

Dobbs, T. A., Smith, A. B., & Taylor, N. J. (2006). "No, we don't get a say, children just suffer the consequences": Children talk about family discipline. *The International Journal of Children's Rights, 14*, 137–156.

Education Counts. (2014). *Annual ECE census report 2014*. Wellington: Ministry of Education.

Education Review Office. (2012). *Partnership with whānau Māori in early childhood services*. Wellington: Author.

Education Review Office. (2013). *Working with Te Whāriki*. Wellington: Author.

Education Review Office. (2015). *Infants and toddlers: Competent and confident communicators and explorers*. Wellington: Author.

Ministry of Education. (1996). *Te whāriki: He whāriki mātauranga mō ngā mokopuna o Aotearoa: Early childhood curriculum*. Wellington: Author.

Ministry of Education. (2015). *Report of the Advisory Group on Early Learning*. Wellington: Ministry of Education.

Ministry of Social Development. (2015). *UNCRC: Fifth periodic report by the Government of New Zealand 2015*. Wellington: Author.

Ministry of Youth Affairs. (1995). *Initial periodic report of New Zealand to the UN Committee on the Rights of the Child*. Wellington: Author.

Ministry of Youth Affairs. (2000). *Second periodic report of New Zealand to the UN Committee on the Rights of the Child*. Wellington: Author.

Ministry of Youth Development. (2008). *Third and fourth periodic report of New Zealand to the UN Committee on the Rights of the Child*. Wellington: Author.

Newell, P. (2011). The human rights imperative to eliminate physical punishment. In J. Durrant & A. B. Smith (Eds.), *Global pathways to abolishing physical punishment: Realising children's rights* (pp. 7–26). New York, NY: Routledge.

Ritchie, J., Harvey, N., Kayes, M., & Smith, C. (2014). *Our children, our choice: Priorities for policy*. Child Poverty Action Group Policy Paper Series Part Two: Early Childhood Care & Education. Auckland: Child Poverty Action Group.

Ritchie, J., & Ritchie, J. (1981). *Spare the rod*. Sydney, NSW: George Allen & Unwin.

Smith, A. B. (1980). A community child care scheme in New Zealand. *Australian Journal of Early Childhood, 5*(2), 26–31.

Smith, A. B. (1993). Early childhood educare: Seeking a theoretical framework in Vygotsky's work. *International Journal of Early Years Education, 1*(1), 47–61.

Smith, A. B. (1996). The quality of childcare centres for infants in New Zealand. *NZARE 'State of the art' monograph No 4*. Palmerston North: NZARE / Department of Policy Studies, Massey University.

Smith, A. B. (2012). *Submission on the Green Paper on Vulnerable Children*. Unpublished submission provided to UNICEF as part of a joint NGO submission.

Smith, A. B. (2013). *Understanding children and childhood* (5th ed.). Wellington: Bridget Williams Books.

Smith, A. B. (2015a). Changing the law on physical punishment in New Zealand. In A. B. Smith (Ed.), *Enhancing children's rights: Connecting research, policy and practice* (pp. 33–47). Basingstoke, UK: Palgrave Macmillan.

Smith, A. B. (2015b). Early childhood education in New Zealand: Progress and challenges in achieving children's rights. In A. B. Smith (Ed.), *Enhancing children's rights: Connecting research, policy and practice* (pp. 80–94). Basingstoke, UK: Palgrave Macmillan.

Smith, A. B. (2016). *Children's rights: Towards social justice*. New York, NY: Momentum Press.

Smith, A. B., Gollop, M. M., Taylor, N. J., & Marshall, K. A. (Eds.). (2005). *The discipline and guidance of children: Messages from research*. Wellington: Office of the Children's Commissioner.

Taylor, N. J., Wood, B., & Smith, A. B. (2011). New Zealand: The achievements and challenges of prohibition. In J. Durrant & A. B. Smith (Eds.), *Global pathways to abolishing physical punishment: Realizing children's rights* (pp. 182–196). New York, NY: Routledge.

Te One, S. (2010). *Early childhood education. New pathways to an uncertain future*. ACYA working paper. Auckland: ACYA.

United Nations Committee on the Rights of the Child. (2005). *General comment No. 7: Implementing child rights in early childhood*. Geneva, Switzerland: UN.

United Nations Committee on the Rights of the Child. (2006). *General comment No. 8: The right of the child to protection from corporal punishment and other degrading punishment.* Geneva, Switzerland: UN.

United Nations Committee on the Rights of the Child. (2011). *General comment No. 13: The right of the child to freedom from all forms of violence.* Geneva, Switzerland: UN.

United Nations Committee on the Rights of the Child. (1997, 2003, 2011, 2016). *Concluding observations of the Committee on the Rights of the Child: New Zealand.* Geneva, Switzerland: UN.

# Chapter 6 Assessment for learning: Promoting children's rights and social justice

Terry Crooks, Grace Grima and Margaret Carr

## Introduction

Assessment for learning approaches are powerful influences on the development and attainment of learners. Teachers and families know this, and research has provided supporting evidence (for example, Black & Wiliam, 1998; Hattie, 2008; Stobart, 2008). Related to both development and attainment, assessment for learning can play a role in supporting and promoting children's rights and social justice. In this chapter we set out five principles of assessment in education that promote learning and, at the same time, support and promote children's rights and social justice, acknowledging the work of Aotearoa New Zealand's Professor Anne Smith.

The first principle is that an assessment practice should describe a learning journey—monitoring progress over time, connecting the past to the present and looking to the future. The second principle flows from this: it is helpful if the learning outcomes to be assessed can take cognisance of a facilitating educational environment and have some consistency across the span of early childhood education and schooling.

The third relates to the contribution of assessment to learner motivation, with self-efficacy as a desired consequence. The fourth is that the assessment practice itself should include a shared process: active participation ensuring assessment is one of the primary means for developing the agency of the learner. Finally, we advocate for, and provide examples of, assessment as effective and trustworthy feedback.

Each principle is introduced with a quotation from Anne Smith's writing. We refer mainly to early years' practice in Aotearoa New Zealand at the present time as a context, although these principles apply to all levels of education.

## Principle 1: An assessment practice should describe a learning journey, monitoring progress over time

> The most important goal of assessment [is] strengthening children's learning identities and their motivation for ongoing learning. The sensitive and informed use of assessment is an important aspect of effective classroom and early childhood practice, because it influences what students think is important to learn, their motivation and their self-belief. (Smith, 2013, p. 257)

Three frames of reference are used in educational assessments: normative, standards-based and ipsative. The normative approach compares the relative performance of different learners: reporting place in class is a familiar example. The standards-based approach compares the performance of each learner to described standards of performance, such as New Zealand's National Standards for primary school performance in reading, writing and mathematics, or some of the standards for awarding NCEA[1] credits in the latter years of secondary education. The ipsative approach compares the current performance of a learner to his or her previous performance, with a clear focus on identifying and describing the extent of progress the learner has made.

To achieve the goal of helping to improve the performance and motivation of every learner, which is our focus here, the most important way of describing assessed performance is to make comparisons with earlier performance (the ipsative approach). When the approach includes positive achievements it can strengthen children's learning identities and their

---

1  National Certificate of Educational Achievement.

motivation for ongoing learning. In early childhood education—and often in schools, too—assessments are housed in individual portfolios, enabling learners, teachers and families to review the learning journey so far; to celebrate progress and consider future actions and endeavours. Some schools have used 'split-screen' analyses to assess both the subject requirements and the key competencies. For examples of the uses of portfolios in schools, see Chetcuti and Grima (2001) and Brady (2004).

Hattie and Timperley (2007, p. 87) state that "to be effective, feedback needs to be clear, purposeful, meaningful and compatible with students' prior knowledge and to provide logical connections". In their model, effective feedback must answer three questions: 'Where am I going?', 'How am I going?' and 'Where to next?' They also caution against what Torrance and Pryor (1998) describe as criteria compliance, whereby ticking off objectives and criteria takes on a greater importance than the learning itself, and where feedback is overly directive. They also make the point that any feedback should be about the student's work rather than the student.

It is important to point out that Hattie and Timperley (2007) found that praise, on its own, was the least effective type of feedback because students could learn nothing from it. Eleanore Hargreaves (2011) writes about provocative feedback which aims to get the learner to think deeply, question him- or herself, have new ideas, reflect on the learning and take action. It encourages learners to self-regulate by discovering for themselves where learning has been successful and to share good strategies with their peers.

## Principle 2: In order to describe a learning journey, it is helpful if learning outcomes to be assessed can take cognisance of a facilitating educational environment and have some consistency across the span of early childhood education and schooling

> Our curriculum in New Zealand is Te Whāriki, published in 1996 and compulsory for registered ECE centers in New Zealand … [It] is based on sociocultural, bicultural, and holistic principles, and has a deliberate focus on incorporating children's and families' voices. (Smith, 2016, p. 56)

The goals and outcomes for early childhood and school-level education in New Zealand are captured in two curriculum documents: for early childhood in *Te Whāriki* (Ministry of Education, 1996) and for school in *The New Zealand Curriculum* (Ministry of Education, 2007). These documents currently retain strong support from the relevant education agencies and professional bodies. They address a wide range of knowledge, skills/competencies, attitudes/values and dispositions. They are unique internationally in that the early childhood strands of outcome in *Te Whāriki* are paralleled in the school curriculum's key competencies. The alignment of the curricula is as follows: wellbeing/managing self, belonging/participating and contributing, exploration/thinking, communication/using language symbols and texts, contribution/relating to others.

The relative emphasis on subject-based and competency-based outcomes and goals is constantly being contested and revisited, however. For instance, the apparent discretion and flexibility that *The New Zealand Curriculum* offered to individual teachers and schools was substantially curtailed by the publishing of National Standards for reading, writing and mathematics and the associated statements about how much of the school week should be devoted to student development in these particular areas. Those new standards and guidelines did not directly contradict statements in the curriculum about the importance of five key competencies, nor did they explicitly devalue learning in other areas of the curriculum. However, they did strongly nudge the balance of the school curriculum towards some goals, and by implication suggest less attention be paid to other goals.

In the early childhood context, the sociocultural, bicultural and holistic framing of *Te Whāriki* insists on the connection between learning and a learning environment. In effect, learning in the early years is described as wellbeing *in*, belonging *to*, exploration *of*, communication *for* and contribution *to*. This acknowledges that it is the child plus the environment that does the learning, consistent with the curriculum principles in *Te Whāriki* that "the early childhood curriculum reflects the holistic ways children learn and grow" and "children learn through responsive and reciprocal relationships with people places and things".

David Perkins (2009) writes in a similar way about a theory of learning as "an integrative theory of action" (p. 18). In the early childhood sector it has been recognised that this relational or integrative defining of aims and objectives in *Te Whāriki* was most accurately translated into assessment by using a narrative format, where the learning and the affordances are assessed together as *learning stories* (Carr & Lee, 2012). Learning stories now support *Te Whāriki* in a range of early childhood programmes, languages and countries (Lee, Carr, Soutar, & Mitchell, 2013). They give strength to the philosophy of assessment *for learning* because they include a 'What next?' that may include the learner, the learning opportunity, or both. Exemplars of these narrative assessments have been published by the Ministry of Education in a series of 20 books (Ministry of Education, 2004, 2005, 2009). More recently, schools have responded to the challenge of combining the demands of subjects and key competencies by using learning stories in the early years, with an eye to the early development of a holistic *learner identity* (Davis, Wright, Carr, & Peters, 2013).

## *Principle 3: Self-efficacy as a desired consequence of assessment*

> Self-efficacy refers to beliefs about one's ability to achieve a task, which influences how hard they try to succeed at a task, how long they persist with it and whether they can achieve the learning outcome. (Smith, 2013, p. 56)

This principle is about paying close attention to individual differences. Three reasons sit behind it: the range of capabilities within most typical groups of learners is very large; good learning progress is most likely to happen when learning activities are appropriate to current levels of capability; and self-efficacy is about motivation.

Even though they may all be of similar age, it is normal to find *some children performing at levels typical of substantially older learners* and others *performing at levels typical of substantially younger learners*. These differences can arise from differences in inherited capabilities or aptitudes, but are at least as likely to arise from differences in life experience. For instance, learners who have been exposed to a rich range of musical experiences, perhaps at home or through community organisations such as churches, are likely to have more advanced capabilities in performing music or responding to music. Similarly, those who have had a lot of experience in playing with balls are likely to be more skilled in such skills as catching, throwing, kicking or hitting balls. Those who have had extensive exposure to a rich range of a language through oral communication, being read to, listening to performances in the language and developing reading skills themselves are likely to be comparatively advanced in skills with that language. These deviations from the average capabilities within a group of learners indicate clearly that assessment of development and learning in each learning domain should begin by assessing the initial capability and performance, and then move on to monitoring and supporting progress from the initial assessment.

Good learning progress is most likely to happen when learning activities are *appropriate to current levels of capability*. Tasks that are already well within the capabilities of a learner are unlikely to promote further learning, while tasks that are far ahead of the current capabilities are more likely to foster frustration rather than growth.

The third reason for paying full attention to individual differences centres on *learner motivation*. Scholars working in this area, such as Carol Dweck (1986, 2006) and Mihaly Csikszentmihalyi (1990, 1997), have identified the strong learning momentum that becomes possible when learners work on tasks they see as quite challenging but not impossible. There is little point in asking a young piano student with quite limited skills to try to learn to perform a Mozart sonata, but for a more advanced student the same request might be a stimulating and rewarding challenge. Motivation is a key consideration in learning and development: little will be achieved without motivation, so creating conditions favourable to learner motivation is a high priority in educational settings.

Anne Smith (2013) elaborated on this point. She referred to Dale Schunk (2004), who described self-efficacy as a subjective perception of what a person thinks they can do in a specific domain, although it is not the same as knowing what to do. She went on to explain that self-efficacy is influenced by past experience, such as teacher expectations and judgements, feedback and modelling (by the teacher or peers). She concluded that choosing a very competent peer is not necessarily the best strategy, because self-efficacy (including notions of resilience and perseverance) is more likely to be enhanced by seeing another person overcome initial struggle. She suggested that other ways in which teachers can improve children's self-efficacy are through encouraging actions or thoughts associated with it.

For all of the reasons above, appropriate recognition of and responsiveness to individual differences is a very high priority and is central to the effectiveness of assessment processes.

## *Principle 4: Assessment as a shared process*

> Children's voices, as well as those of their families, are included in learning stories allowing children to share meanings and ownership of their learning. Children's rights, to express and share their views (Articles 12 and 13 [in the United Nations Convention on the Rights of the Child]), are embedded in *Te Whāriki*, and it provides an excellent model of a curriculum that incorporates children's participation rights. (Smith, 2016, p. 56)

Much of the literature on testing and assessment appears to regard them as activities that teachers do to their students. But here, where we are talking about assessment as a way of promoting educational quality, that is too limited a view. Successful assessment procedures use enhanced feedback, encourage students to be actively involved in the learning, use assessment results to enhance learning and teaching, and support learners towards self-assessment (Black, Harrison, Lee, Marshall, & William, 2003; Clarke, Timperley, & Hattie, 2001).

A core ingredient of assessment that helps development and learning is the active participation of the learners. The most influential scholar in developing and promoting this idea has been Royce Sadler. In his seminal paper in 1989 he emphasised that the active involvement of learners in self-assessment is a vital component of effective assessment for learning and development. For useful change to happen, a learner needs both to recognise the desirability of change and to begin to see how to change. Clearly, teachers and peers can help with both of these requirements, but self-recognition and self-commitment are vital ingredients for effective change. Wynne Harlen and Mary James (1997) have summarised Sadler's point nicely:

> pupils have to be active in their own learning (teachers cannot learn for them) and unless they come to understand their own strengths and weaknesses, and how they might deal with them, they will not make progress. (p. 372)

Becoming proficient in self-assessment has two main requirements: developing understanding of the qualities that are associated with good or excellent performances in the tasks or area concerned, and developing skills in identifying how well those qualities are shown in one's own work. Converting these building blocks into improved performance requires a third element: the motivation/commitment to make the effort to bridge any gaps between the current performance and the recognised qualities that should be sought. Dylan Wiliam (2009) refers to a colleague from Kings' College who used to refer to "plenty of formative intention but relatively little formative action" (p. 9). This observation, which applies to both learners and teachers, differentiates between the intention to take action and actually taking the necessary action to improve performance.

Isaacs, Zara, Herbert, Coombs and Smith (2013) support the view that continuous assessment can provide a holistic approach to assessment as well as immediate and effective feedback to both the learner and the practitioner about the learner's strengths and areas that need further development. They also point out that:

> such an approach requires a commitment from all staff to the implementation of the approach in an agreed format. Staff need to be skilled users of a variety of assessment instruments, skilled interpreters of the evidence that is generated and skilled recorders of the data. Staff may need training in the use and implementation of such systems. (p. 36)

John Hattie (2008) and Hattie and Timperley (2007) have shown that educators can play a key role in promoting development and learning through their feedback on learners' work. Provided that learners want to perform better, such feedback can serve two key functions: to help learners better understand what a good performance looks like, and to help them identify the aspects of their current work that need improvement. If these conditions are met, there is a strong chance that improvement will follow.

There are usually further important players in the learning environment: the other learners. There is strong evidence (Nuthall, 1999; Alton-Lee, Nuthall, & Patrick, 1993) that the observations and feedback offered by peers can play a strong role in learning and development.

Their affirmations and suggestions can be very helpful. On the other hand, their negative comments can undermine the conditions that favour motivation and progress.

Particularly with younger children, parents and other family members are further powerful influences on progress in learning and development. Their interest, time committed and responses to what learners are doing are often important signals to the learners about the importance and merit of what they have been working on and can reinforce or undermine the influence of teachers and peers.

## *Principle 5: Effective feedback and guidance includes trustworthiness*

> Quality is deeply embedded in the engagement of adults and children together, but from a rights perspective, the core aspect of quality is listening to children's voice and perspectives and taking them seriously. (Smith, 2016, p. 59)

Effective guidance requires an atmosphere of trust. Learners receiving guidance from an educator or a peer will respond most positively to that guidance if they trust the person who is offering it. They need to be confident that the person genuinely cares about them and has their interests at heart. This allows them to reveal the difficulties or doubts they are having, and therefore to maximise opportunities for their helpers to understand their needs and offer really useful help.

Usually, effective guidance has the character of a conversation. There is clear evidence that learners are more open to feedback if they are able to explain why they have done what they have done, and to indicate what they think they have done well, indifferently or poorly. This gives the person offering guidance clues to what will be most appropriate to say to help the person they are guiding. Few of us enjoy simply being told what to do, without any sense of personal agency or control!

Guidance is most effective if it is offered when learners receiving the guidance are actively engaged with the tasks on which they are receiving feedback and feel they can receive tangible benefit from paying attention to the guidance and acting upon it. This is especially the case when the learning activity is part of an extended sequence of similar work, so that there will be multiple opportunities to incorporate improvements into the learning activities and products.

A 3-year longitudinal observational and interview study of 4- and 5-year-olds (in their New Zealand childhood centres and schools), entitled Learning in the Making, was co-authored by Anne Smith. This study used episodes of 10 minutes or more as "thematic or functional" units of analysis to analyse the development of dispositional learning over time (a way of including, in research, the learners together with the affordances). We quote from this book to illustrate principle 5:

> The teachers' efforts to know all the children well and develop relationships with them invited their engagement and interest in activities at the centre. Teachers and their attitudes, and their facilitation of children's projects, were a key aspect of the affordance network. David, for example, was able to build on the early childhood teacher's belief that children can take responsibility for their own learning. (Carr, Smith, Duncan, Jones, Lee, & Marshall, 2010, p. 117)

## Concluding comments

This chapter has discussed formative assessment with a focus on the early years, and has used examples from Aotearoa New Zealand. Formative assessment is about evoking information about learning and using that information to improve learning (Black et al., 2003, p. 122), and we have argued that five considerations (described as principles) should accompany the formative role of assessment if a key purpose of education is deemed to be social justice and children's rights. There is no better scholarly work for enunciating that key purpose than the writing of Anne B. Smith. Her 2016 book was entitled *Children's Rights: Towards Social Justice*. That book concludes with a quote from John Tobin (2011, p. 89):

> The mainstreaming of children's rights is a deeply political project with potentially transformative consequences for the way in which children are engaged with by all actors in society.

We agree, and we suggest that the way we assess children in education is a key site for working on that project.

## References

Alton-Lee, A. G., Nuthall, G. A., & Patrick, J. (1993). Reframing classroom research: A lesson from the private world of children. *Harvard Educational Review, 63*(1), 50–84.

Black, P., Harrison, C., Lee, C., Marshall, B., & Wiliam, D. (2003). *Assessment for learning: Putting it into practice.* Maidenhead, UK: Open University Press.

Black, P., & Wiliam, D. (1998). Assessment and classroom learning. *Assessment in Education, 5,* 7-74.

Brady, L. (2004). Portfolios in schools: A longitudinal study. *Journal of Educational Enquiry, 5*(2), 116–128.

Carr, M., & Lee, W. (2012). *Learning stories: Constructing learner identities in early education.* London, UK: Sage.

Carr, M., Smith, A. B., Duncan, J., Jones, C., Lee, W., & Marshall, K. (2010). *Learning in the making: Disposition and design in early education.* Rotterdam, The Netherlands: Sense Publishers.

Chetcuti, D., & Grima, G. (2001). *Portfolio assessment.* Malta: National Curriculum Council, Ministry of Education.

Clarke, S., Timperley, H., & Hattie, J. (2001). *Unlocking formative assessment: Practical strategies for enhancing students' learning in the primary and intermediate classroom.* London, UK: Holder and Stoughton.

Csikszentmihalyi, M. (1990). Literacy and intrinsic motivation. *Daedalus, 119*(2), 115–140.

Csikszentmihalyi, M. (1997). *Finding flow: The psychology of engagement with everyday life.* New York, NY: Basic Books.

Davis, K., Wright, J., Carr, M., & Peters, S. (2013). *Key competencies, assessment and learning stories: Talking with teachers and students.* [Book with introduction and workshops, and DVD]. Wellington: NZCER Press.

Dweck, C. (1986). Motivational processes affecting learning. *American Psychologist, 41*(10), 1040–1048.

Dweck, C. (2006). *Mindset: The new psychology of success.* New York, NY: Random House.

Hargreaves, E. (2011). Teachers' classroom feedback: Still trying to get it right. *Pedagogies: An International Journal, 7*(1), 1–15.

Harlen, W., & James, M. (1997). Assessment and learning: Differences and relationships between formative and summative assessment. *Assessment in Education, 4*(3), 365–379.

Hattie, J. (2008). *Visible learning*. London, UK: Routledge.

Hattie, J., & Timperley, H. (2007). The power of feedback. *Review of Educational Research, 77*, 81–112.

Isaacs, T., Zara, C., Herbert, G., Coombs, S. J., & Smith, C. (2013). *Key concepts in educational assessment*. London, UK: Sage.

Lee, W., Carr, M., Soutar, B., & Mitchell, L. (2013). *Understanding the Te Whāriki approach: Early years education in practice*. Oxon, UK: Routledge.

Ministry of Education. (1996). *Te whāriki: He whāriki mātauranga mō ngā mokopuna o Aotearoa: Early childhood curriculum*. Wellington: Author.

Ministry of Education. (2004, 2005, 2009). *Kei tua o te pae: Assessment for learning: Early childhood exemplars* [20 booklets]. Wellington: Learning Media.

Ministry of Education. (2007). *The New Zealand curriculum*. Wellington: Learning Media.

Nuthall, G. A. (1999). Learning how to learn: The evolution of students' minds through the social processes and culture of the classroom. *International Journal of Educational Research, 31*(3), 139–256 [whole issue].

Perkins, D. N. (2009). *Making learning whole: How seven principles of teaching can transform education*. San Francisco, CA: Jossey-Bass.

Sadler, D. R. (1989). Formative assessment and the design of instructional systems. *Instructional Science, 18*, 119–144.

Schunk, D. H. (2004). *Learning theories: An educational perspective* (4th ed.). Upper Saddle River, NJ: Pearson.

Smith, A. B. (2013). *Understanding children and childhood* (5th ed.). Wellington: Bridget Williams Books.

Smith, A. B. (2016). *Children's Rights: Towards social justice*. New York, NY: Momentum Press, LLC.

Stobart, G. (2008). *Testing times: The uses and abuses of assessment*. London, UK: Routledge.

Tobin, J. (2011). Understanding a human rights based approach to matters involving children: Conceptual foundations and strategic considerations. In A. Invernizzi & J. Williams (Eds.), *The human rights of children: From visions to implementation* (pp. 61–98). London, UK: Routledge.

Torrance, H., & Pryor, J. (1998). *Investigating formative assessment: Teaching, learning and assessment in the classroom*. Philadelphia, PA: Open University Press.

Wiliam, D. (2009). *Assessment for learning: Why, what and how?: An inaugural professorial lecture.* London, UK: Institute of Education, University of London.

# Chapter 7  Children's rights and social justice: An analysis of Anne B. Smith's contribution

Mark Henaghan

### *Introduction*

Professor Anne Smith was at the forefront of the children's rights movement in New Zealand for several decades. Her energy and passion for making the world a better place for children was inspirational, and she was tireless in her call for children's rights and place in society to be better recognised. Her advocacy for children's voices to be listened to and respected, and for children to be protected from all forms of physical violence—including that inflicted under the guise of discipline—contributed to the societal shift that made possible the repeal of section 59 of the Crimes Act in 2007. This is particularly important work in a society where children have no individual political power of their own and are solely reliant on adults to improve their position.

This chapter examines Smith's significant life-long contribution to children's rights from a legal perspective, primarily focusing on her important and inspirational child-focused book *Children's Rights: Towards Social Justice* (Smith, 2016) and the United Nations Convention on the Rights of the Child (the UNCRC). It is very rare to read a book where you cannot find anything with which to disagree and where every page puts a smile on your face. This was my experience reading Smith's book. On every page her compassion and care for children as precious independent beings making their way in the world are abundantly clear. The term 'independent being' means that each child, no matter what their age, has their own unique way of seeing and experiencing their world in conjunction with their families, their friends, and the societies in which they live.

Children have the right to be respected, accepted and listened to on their own terms. This does not mean that adults should cater to children's every wish and desire. However, we need to recognise that every child who comes into this world is irreplaceable and is imbued with unique potential that should be developed to the maximum degree possible. Interactions with children should provide the framework for this to happen.[1] This idea is at the heart of Smith's idea of social justice. It is an approach that respects children and their individual rights, and that ultimately fosters societies of well-developed, independent-thinking citizens. Children who are respected, heard and nurtured generally grow into adults who will ensure such respect and nurturing is passed on to the next generation.

The benefits of a just society based on this view of social justice and children's rights are supported by empirical evidence. Richard Wilkinson and Kate Pickett demonstrate that more equal societies are economically better off, have fewer social problems and are more satisfying to live in (Wilkinson & Pickett, 2009). The world-renowned Dunedin Multidisciplinary Health and Development Study, which continues to gather information on the lives of 1,037 children born in Dunedin, New Zealand, between 1 April 1972 and 31 March 1973, provides ample evidence that the early years of a child's life have a major impact on the rest of their lives.[2]

A society that adheres to the children's rights model advocated by Smith would give children the best possible start in life. *Children's Rights: Towards Social Justice* should be compulsory reading for all politicians, aspiring politicians, early childhood and school teachers, policy makers, and all those who wish to make the world a better place.

## Children's rights within families

Most children are born into some kind of family, in all its many possible configurations. Smith rightly starts her analysis of children's rights by considering their place within the family. Families have a massive influence on the children within them, especially in the early years of children's lives. Jim Flynn's book, *Does Your Family Make You Smarter?: Nature, Nurture, and Human Autonomy*, shows that a child's vocabulary is formed within their family and has a large influence on the rest of their life, especially in terms of the child's future opportunities (Flynn, 2016).

A framework based on the rights of children within their families provides children with particular guarantees. As Smith (2016, p. 24) explained, giving children rights within families is a controversial position to take. Families are seen as private and beyond legal influence, with parents having the 'right' to bring up their children as they see fit (ibid.). However, the full dependence of very young children upon their family for their survival and development and children's lack of control over their lives means that the rights and interests of children within their families need to be protected.

Smith identified four key principles underpinning the UNCRC that provide a framework for the family life of children (Smith, 2016, p. 26). First, the principle of non-discrimination means that children should not be discriminated against based on the type of family they live in. It also means that within families children should not be discriminated against and their rights should be respected "regardless of their age, sex, temperament, disability, sexuality, or ethnicity" (ibid.).

The second principle is that the best interests of children must be a primary consideration when decisions are made about children within families (ibid.). This is encapsulated in Article 3 of the UNCRC,[3] and in section 4 of New Zealand's domestic legislation: the Care of Children Act 2004.[4] The best interests of children do not override all other interests, but their interests must be placed high on the agenda.

Third, children have a right to be "protected from harm and nurtured in a way that supports their well-being and ongoing development" (ibid.).[5] This is the primary responsibility of families. As Smith noted (ibid., p. 33):

The UNCRC is clear in its support of family relationships based on happiness, love, and understanding rather than power and authority, while acknowledging that families should provide appropriate direction and guidance for children.

However, parents are not solely responsible for providing an adequate standard of living for children. As Smith argued, "[t]o a large extent families are dependent on their governments to maintain the conditions for them to provide for their children" (Smith, 2016, p. 35). Indeed, the UNCRC exerts pressure on governments to provide adequate support for families, particularly where economic conditions mean that some families are not able to provide the basics of adequate food and shelter for their children (ibid., p. 24). This is particularly topical in New Zealand, where 305,000 children were estimated to be living in poverty in 2015 (Simpson, Duncanson, Oben, Wicken, & Pierson, 2015). These children are not likely to obtain adequate standards of living without government support. It is clear that more needs to be done to support these children.[6]

Smith extended this principle of protection from harm to cover physical discipline and has been an international tower of strength in advocating for a world where all children are free from physical punishment (Smith, 2005, 2015). Smith acknowledged that although there is no specific mention of corporal punishment in the UNCRC, the Committee on the Rights of the Child generally "regards corporal punishment as a violation of children's rights" and says "it disapproves of the continuing legal and social acceptance of its use" (Smith, 2016, p. 33). Every year fewer countries legally justify the physical punishment of children. Smith reported that, as at November 2015, 47 states in the world prohibited all forms of corporal punishment of children (including within the home) and "another 51 [were] committed to law reform" (ibid.). These figures show how far the world has come in this regard. Smith pointed out that in 1979 only Sweden prohibited the physical punishment of children, and when the UNCRC was created in 1989 only eight countries banned this practice (ibid.). As she rightly noted, "[t]he decline in the use of physical punishment is a sign of increasing respect for democratic values and children's citizenship, and the importance of collective responsibility for children's well-being"

(Smith, 2016, p. 34). Within this international movement, Smith was a tireless trailblazer, especially in terms of her research illustrating that children have negative feelings about being physically punished (Smith, 2015).

The final fundamental right of children within families is the right to participate in family life (Smith, 2016, p. 26).[7] This is not only important in terms of children being respected as individuals within the family; it is also important in establishing a just society. A just society listens to the voices of everyone within that society, regardless of their status or position. A just society does not rule from the top down, but is much more inclusive (Acemoğlu & Robinson, 2012). Acemoğlu and Robinson's book *Why Nations Fail: The Origins of Power, Prosperity, and Poverty* demonstrates the link between inclusive economics, political institutions and prosperity. As the authors say, "[i]nclusive economic institutions are in turn supported by, and support, inclusive political institutions, that is, those that distribute political power widely in a pluralistic manner" (p. 424). This ethos of inclusion starts with the family in the early years of childhood. It does not mean that children must always get their own way: as in all 'mini democracies', the most individuals can expect is to be heard alongside the voices of others. Children's views need to be taken into account, but their views will not always prevail.

Smith made a major contribution to children being heard through her research on children's perspectives on contact with their parents after separation (Smith & Gollop, 2001; Smith, Taylor, & Tapp, 2003). This research reveals what it feels like to be a powerless child surrounded by conflict. This work has helped families and Family Court professionals pay more attention to what is happening to the children concerned rather than focusing on what the adults are saying about each other.

## Children's rights within early childhood education and care services

Anne Smith also made a significant international contribution to establishing the importance of children's rights in the context of early childhood education and care settings, an area she had worked in since the 1970s (Smith, 1997, 1999, 2007; Smith, Grima, Gaffney, & Powell, 2000). Smith was keenly aware that:

Children usually have their first sustained experiences outside a family environment within early childhood education and care services, and these experiences can be a potent force in achieving social justice and rights for young children. (Smith, 2016, p. 45)

Smith used the principles from the UNCRC of participation, universalism, best interests and the right to survival and development to provide a framework for high-quality early childhood education, which is essential for the development of children (ibid., pp. 45–49). Her views support the argument by Barnett and Ackerman (2006, p. 51) that high-quality early childhood education is the best investment a society can make in terms of the "educational, social and economic success of children growing up in disadvantaged circumstances".

Smith advocated for a view of early childhood education based on children as "active co-constructors of knowledge and culture, with their own identity as people and learners" (Anning, 2004, p. 59),[8] and where even the youngest children have "a say in decisions about routine, pace, and control" (Pugh & Selleck, 1996).[9] This fits well with her strong philosophy of ensuring children are given the maximum opportunity to find their own voice and be active participants in their understanding of the world (Smith, 2016, p. 65). Such an approach results in children who are confident and who take responsibility for their own learning.

## *Children's rights at school*

School is a large part of children's lives. Smith (2016, pp. 67–88) identified five fundamental rights associated with education: (i) access to school; (ii) protection from violence at school; (iii) protection from exclusion from school; (iv) protection from discrimination at school; and (v) participation rights at school. If children are denied access to education they are likely to suffer disadvantages for the rest of their lives. Exclusion from school is a serious violation of children's rights. Smith (ibid., p. 80) argued that:

> The process of excluding children from school as a disciplinary measure is problematic from a children's rights perspective. Exclusion policies violate all four of the UNCRC principles and are part of a punitive discourse about consequences for children. Children are seen

as problems in need of discipline, rather than respected as developing human beings with rights to education, justice, and the affirmation of their dignity.

Exclusion clearly has a negative impact on children and can also be extremely discriminatory in practice. Smith (ibid., p. 81) further stated:

> Exclusion policies do not support the best interests of the child because they have many long-term negative outcomes for children, and they are discriminatory because poor children, disabled children, and children from minority racial groups are more likely to be excluded. Children's survival and development rights are diminished by exclusion, as it can lead to a downward spiral of dropout from education, unemployment, antisocial behaviour, and even imprisonment.

Any time out of school also inevitably puts a child behind other children in terms of their development and abilities to learn. Some schools have developed alternative strategies to exclusion to deal with bad behaviour, and Smith offered examples of creative solutions such as providing spaces within schools to work with those children on "building respectful relationships, fostering a sense of belonging … encouraging and developing self-efficacy, and … develop[ing] a sense of purpose" (ibid., pp. 82–83).

In line with one of the major themes of her research, Smith strongly emphasised children's participation rights at school. As she said, Article 12 (the right to express views) and Article 13 (the right to give and receive information) of the UNCRC "are pivotal to children's participation rights" (ibid., p. 85). Smith carried out a significant study of children's educational participation and found that 96 per cent of 16-year-old secondary school students in the study (n = 721) "wanted to be allowed to express their opinion about things that affected them (such as choosing subjects, school camps, school trips, dress codes)". However, in reality very few of the students (just 13 percent) felt they had an opportunity to express their views on such matters (ibid., p. 86).

When children participate in what is happening at school, and when their views are respected and taken into account, they are much more likely to care about their school. The unique perspective of the children as the individuals actually attending the school can also be extremely valuable in pointing to new and different ways in which the experience of school may be enhanced for themselves and for others. Although there have been improvements in the way that, as a society, we listen to children at school—for example, by having student representatives on school boards of trustees—Smith's research has shown that such participation can still be unsatisfactory when children are not listened to adequately and when one student's voice is not necessarily heard (ibid., pp. 87–88).

## *Children's rights in child protection systems*

Article 19 of the UNCRC gives children the right to be free from "all forms of physical or mental violence, injury or abuse, neglect or negligent treatment, maltreatment or exploitation, including sexual abuse".[10] Child abuse of any kind has major consequences for children and it should be avoided at all costs. Smith noted that discourses of risk and vulnerability are often used when describing children who have been abused (Smith, 2016, p. 94). However, such discourses tend to "decrease children's resilience", which turns children into permanent victims of others, rather than providing them with support to develop resilience and their own ways of coping (ibid., p. 95).

Smith observed that "managerialistic" approaches to child protection do not work and have a dramatically negative effect on children's well-being (ibid., p. 99). Such approaches focus on "standardization and e-technology" rather than direct contact with families and children (ibid.). The set performance targets employed limits the amount of time social workers can spend with individual families and children. Eradicating child abuse is not simply a matter of investigating and recording data, but of building a strong, supportive connection with the child and family concerned. This takes time and significant resources. However, there are no shortcuts to dealing with such a significant intergenerational problem.[11]

In terms of children living in state care, Smith also believed that the government has an obligation to ensure children are in "good, secure alternative care arrangements" (ibid., p. 101).[12] This involves giving significantly more thought to recognising the important role of foster parents when children are unable to be cared for within their own families, and listening to what it is like to be a child in state care. These children have less opportunity to participate in decision-making about their lives, which are controlled by bureaucratic processes rather than listening to individual children.

Attention also needs to be given to preventive measures to reduce the number of families needing state intervention in the first place. Smith used the Victorian Maternal and Child Health Services as a successful example of a preventive public health initiative involving the creation of small parent groups covering 98 percent of infants born in Victoria (ibid., p. 109). These groups provide support to first-time parents. The research shows that after 2 years, 80 percent of the parent groups were still operating and had become self-sustaining, frequently resulting in "lifelong friendships" (ibid.).

## Children's rights to health

Article 24 of the UNCRC guarantees children the right "to the enjoyment of the highest attainable standard of health". As Smith (2016, p. 115) noted, "[s]ocial factors during childhood have a profound effect on health throughout life, but their effect is particularly powerful in the first few years of life". Children who live in difficult circumstances also suffer far more health interventions and consequences than other children.[13] It is therefore essential to prioritise infant and maternal health care for those most economically deprived—not just to uphold children's rights, but also for the greater good of society (Expert Advisory Group on Solutions to Child Poverty, 2012). Smith emphasised that children should participate in managing their own health and be given sufficient information about how best to look after their health (Smith, 2016, pp. 121–125).

## Children's rights in the workplace

Historically, children have been exploited in the workforce as cheap labour. Smith pointed out that children worked for their families in Roman times and throughout the Middle Ages (Smith, 2016, p. 134), and that it was not until the 18th century that the negative effects of children working long hours began to be recognised (ibid.). Smith described the history of childhood as "converting children from earners to learners" (ibid., p. 135). New Zealand currently has no legislated minimum age for children to be allowed to begin work, but there are "restrictions on dangerous and hazardous work and working during school hours" (ibid., p. 139).

Children contribute a great deal to the productivity of the world, often in invisible ways. In developing countries children are essential to economic wellbeing and survival. This is reflected in the differences in the childhood experiences of children from such countries compared with those in the more affluent Western world (ibid., p. 152). As Smith rightly stated, we should be campaigning for a world that ensures all children are protected from work that is dangerous, harmful to their health, or exploitative (ibid.). Children also have the right to ensure that paid work does not prevent them from going to school (ibid, p. 153). Children should also be permitted to express their views about work and working conditions, and these views should be taken "seriously" (ibid.).

## Conclusion

Anne Smith's book *Children's Rights: Towards Social Justice* is focused on the importance of the UNCRC and its provision of a universal framework for ensuring children enjoy the best conditions and childhoods possible. The most inspirational theme of the book is that childhood is not a fixed concept, but rather is constructed by the different societies children live in. The constructed nature of childhood means that all societies have the opportunity to improve the childhoods of the children who live within them and to give children more freedom to develop their own unique identities and ways of seeing and experiencing the world.

Smith's book is not simply about childhood: it is about creating a society where everyone is given the chance to flourish and maximise their potential. Smith's work in this field leaves a formidable legacy.

## References

Acemoğlu, D., & Robinson, J. (2012). *Why nations fail: The origins of power, prosperity, and poverty*. London, UK: Profile Books.

Anning, A. (2004). The co-construction of an early childhood curriculum. In A, Anning, J. Cullen, & M. Fleer (Eds.), *Early childhood education: Society and culture*. (pp. 67–79). London, UK: Sage Publications.

Barnett, W. S., & Ackerman, D. (2006). Costs, benefits, and long-term effects of early care and education programs: Recommendations and cautions for community developers. *Community Development, 37*(3), 86.

Children's Commissioner: We're a country of extremes, we're a country of inequality. (2016, 10 July). *One News*. TVNZ. Retrieved from http://www.tvnz.co.nz/one-news.

Dunedin Multidisciplinary Health and Development Research Unit. (2016). *The Dunedin Multidisciplinary Health and Development Study*. Retrieved from http://dunedinstudy.otago.ac.nz/studies

Expert Advisory Group on Solutions to Child Poverty. (2012). *Solutions to child poverty in New Zealand: Evidence for action*. Wellington: Author.

Flynn, J. (2016). *Does your family make you smarter? Nature, nurture, and human autonomy*. Cambridge, UK: Cambridge University Press.

Henaghan, M., & Ballantyne, R. (2015). Child poverty in New Zealand: A contravention of Articles 6 and 27 of the Convention on the Rights of the Child 1989. *Stellenbosch Law Review, 26*(2), 380–398.

Price, R. (2016, 18 August). New 'Ministry for Vulnerable Children' boss to lead culture change, Tolley says. *Stuff News*. Retrieved from http://www.stuff.co.nz.

Pugh, G., & Selleck, D. (1996). Listening to and communicating with young children. In R. Davie, G. Upton, & V. Varma *The voice of the child: A handbook for professionals*. London, UK: The Falmer Press.

Simpson, J., Duncanson, M., Oben, G., Wicken, A., & Pierson, M. (2015). *Child poverty monitor 2015*. Dunedin: New Zealand Child and Youth Epidemiology Service, University of Otago.

Smith, A. (1997). How do we ensure the best interests of children in out-of-home care? Messages from research. *Childrenz Issues, 1*(1), 23.

Smith, A. (1999). Quality childcare and joint attention. *International Journal of Early Years Education, 7*(1), 85.

Smith, A. (2005). Effective discipline and supporting change. In A. Smith, M. Gollop, N. Taylor, & K. Marshall (Eds.), *The discipline and guidance of children: Messages from research*. Wellington: Office of the Commissioner for Children.

Smith, A. (2007). Children and young people's participation rights in education. *International Journal of Children's Rights, 15*(1), 147.

Smith, A. (2015). Changing the law on physical punishment in New Zealand. In A. Smith (Ed.), *Enhancing children's rights: Connecting research, policy, and practice*. Basingstoke, UK: Palgrave MacMillan.

Smith, A. (2016). *Children's rights: Towards social justice*. New York, NY: Momentum Press.

Smith, A., & Gollop, M. (2001). What children think separating parents should know. *New Zealand Journal of Psychology, 30*(1), 23.

Smith, A., Grima, G., Gaffney, M., & Powell, K. (2000). *Early childhood education: Report to the Ministry of Education*. Dunedin: Children's Issues Centre, University of Otago.

Smith, A., Taylor, N., & Tapp, P. (2013). Rethinking children's involvement in decision-making after parental separation. *Childhood, 10*(2), 203.

Vygotsky, L. S. (1980). *Mind in society: The development of higher psychological processes*. Cambridge, MA: Harvard University Press.

Wilkinson, R., & Pickett, K. (2009). *The spirit level: Why greater equality makes societies stronger*. New York, NY: Bloomsbury Press.

Wills, R. (2015). *State of care 2015*. Wellington: Office of the Children's Commissioner.

## *Acknowledgements*

Thank you to Ruth Ballantyne, Professional Practice Fellow, Faculty of Law, University of Otago, Dunedin, New Zealand, for her editorial assistance with this chapter.

## *Endnotes*

1 This is referred to by psychologist Lev Vygotsky as the "zone of proximal development". (See Vygotsky, 1980, pp. 84–91).

2 See http://dunedinstudy.otago.ac.nz/studies.

3 Article 3 of the UNCRC states:

  1. In all actions concerning children, whether undertaken by public or private social welfare institutions, courts of law, administrative authorities or legislative bodies, the best interests of the child shall be a primary consideration.
  2. States Parties undertake to ensure the child such protection and care as is necessary for his or her well-being, taking into account the rights and duties of his or her parents, legal guardians, or other individuals legally responsible for him or her, and, to this end, shall take all appropriate legislative and administrative measures.
  3. States Parties shall ensure that the institutions, services and facilities responsible for the care or protection of children shall conform with the standards established by competent authorities, particularly in the areas of safety, health, in the number and suitability of theihr staff, as well as competent supervision.

4 Section 4(1) of the Care of Children Act 2004 states:
4 Child's welfare and best interests to be paramount

(1) The welfare and best interests of a child in his or her particular circumstances must be the first and paramount consideration—
(a) in the administration and application of this Act, for example, in proceedings under this Act; and
(b) in any other proceedings involving the guardianship of, or the role of providing day-to-day care for, or contact with, a child.

5   Article 6.2 of the UNCRC declares, "States Parties shall ensure to the maximum extent possible the survival and development of the child." Article 18 of the UNCRC states:

1. States Parties shall use their best efforts to ensure recognition of the principle that both parents have common responsibilities for the upbringing and development of the child. Parents or, as the case may be, legal guardians, have the primary responsibility for the upbringing and development of the child. The best interests of the child will be their basic concern.
2. For the purpose of guaranteeing and promoting the rights set forth in the present Convention, States Parties shall render appropriate assistance to parents and legal guardians in the performance of their child-rearing responsibilities and shall ensure the development of institutions, facilities and services for the care of children.
3. States Parties shall take all appropriate measures to ensure that children of working parents have the right to benefit from child-care services and facilities for which they are eligible.

Likewise, Article 19 of the UNCRC states:

1. States Parties shall take all appropriate legislative, administrative, social and educational measures to protect the child from all forms of physical or mental violence, injury or abuse, neglect or negligent treatment, maltreatment or exploitation, including sexual abuse, while in the care of parent(s), legal guardian(s) or any other person who has the care of the child.
2. Such protective measures should, as appropriate, include effective procedures for the establishment of social programmes to provide necessary support for the child and for those who have the care of the child, as well as for other forms of prevention and for identification, reporting, referral, investigation, treatment and follow-up of instances of child maltreatment described heretofore, and, as appropriate, for judicial involvement.

6   New Zealand's current Children's Commissioner, Judge Andrew Becroft, acknowledged New Zealand's significant child poverty problem and called for a collaborative response after his first week in the job as Children's Commissioner. See Children's Commissioner: We're a Country of Extremes, We're a Country of Inequality, 2016. See also Henaghan & Ballantyne, 2015.

7   Article 12 of the UNCRC states:

1. States Parties shall assure to the child who is capable of forming his or her own views the right to express those views freely in all matters affecting the child, the views of the child being given due weight in accordance with the age and maturity of the child.

2. For this purpose, the child shall in particular be provided the opportunity to be heard in any judicial and administrative proceedings affecting the child, either directly, or through a representative or an appropriate body, in a manner consistent with the procedural rules of national law.

Likewise, s 6 of the Care of Children Act 2004 states:

**6. Child's views**

(1) This subsection applies to proceedings involving—

(a) the guardianship of, or the role of providing day-to-day care for, or contact with, a child; or

(b) the administration of property belonging to, or held in trust for, a child; or

(c) the application of the income of property of that kind.

(2) In proceedings to which subsection (1) applies,—

(a) a child must be given reasonable opportunities to express views on matters affecting the child; and

(b) any views the child expresses (either directly or through a representative) must be taken into account.

8   See also Smith, 2016, p. 54.

9   See also Smith, 2016, p. 54.

10  Article 19 of the UNCRC states:

1. States Parties shall take all appropriate legislative, administrative, social and educational measures to protect the child from all forms of physical or mental violence, injury or abuse, neglect or negligent treatment, maltreatment or exploitation, including sexual abuse, while in the care of parent(s), legal guardian(s) or any other person who has the care of the child.

2. Such protective measures should, as appropriate, include effective procedures for the establishment of social programmes to provide necessary support for the child and for those who have the care of the child, as well as for other forms of prevention and for identification, reporting, referral, investigation, treatment and follow-up of instances of child maltreatment described heretofore, and, as appropriate, for judicial involvement.

11  This is a particularly apt time to discuss such changes as New Zealand's child protection agency, Child, Youth and Family, will be disestablished in April 2017 and will be replaced by a new Ministry for Vulnerable Children, Oranga Tamariki. See Price, 2016.

12  The former Children's Commissioner, Dr Russell Wills, discovered that many children living in state care suffered abuse and neglect. This needs to change to ensure children are safe in state care and adequately taken care of. See Wills, 2015.

13  See Dunedin Multidisciplinary Health and Development Research Unit, 2016; Simpson et al., 2015; Expert Advisory Group on Solutions to Child Poverty, 2012.

# Chapter 8 Leaders as advocates in early childhood education: Building capacity for change through development of everyday practice

Joce Nuttall

## *Introduction*

Despite the rapid growth of policy development in early childhood education around the globe, advocacy for the rights of young children to experience high quality, safe and culturally responsive extra-familial environments is as important now as it has always been. These environments are not confined to early childhood education and care services. Children are found in public spaces, health care settings, prisons, and churches—indeed, almost the full range of environments accessed by adults—and their safety and their right to have their perspectives taken into account is a constant across these settings. Increasingly, children also inhabit digital environments, sometimes designed for them and sometimes not. Each of these environments has the potential to surprise, delight and educate, or to negatively affect children's wellbeing and learning. Professionals who choose to work with young children take on a particular duty in relation to advocacy for children across these environments.

In this chapter I express my appreciation of the legacy of Professor Anne Smith in relation to advocacy for children through a particular entry point: the role of leaders in early childhood education and care in taking action for children. My focus is on educators who lead early childhood systems at the level of an individual centre.

## *Leadership as taking action for children*

My research is concerned with centres as workplace systems and the impact leaders can have on children's lives by fostering system-level changes in day-to-day work activities. Reviewers of my work have sometimes critiqued this focus as "insignificant" or "practical". I reject this critique, since it assumes a knowledge hierarchy in which abstract concepts such as values and identity assume a higher status than concrete instantiations of teachers' work. I interpret this critique as an attempt to alienate knowledge from practice, a dichotomy that, as a researcher in an applied field, I fundamentally reject. I accept that phenomena such as values and identity are ontologically real (at least in their effects) and epistemologically important. But the idea that abstracted knowledge or values *precede* the concrete nature of everyday practice (and are therefore superior as well as necessary precursors to practice) should be challenged by everyone with an interest in the work of teachers.

Sociocultural and cultural-historical interpretations of learning and development hold that abstraction and concretion develop *together* in dynamic ways. Ideally, this dynamic gives rise to processes of consciousness raising that allow teachers to continually re-concretise their work in the form of practices that lead to even richer learning for the children in their care. It is at this level of practice that the children and families with whom we work encounter us: as people who *take action*, not as disembodied identities or philosophies, even as these identities and philosophies develop within and alongside everyday practice. My work (Nuttall, 2013) seeks to build, with educational leaders in early childhood settings, approaches to leadership that stimulate consciousness raising about practice, with the ultimate aim of developing ethical and transformative practices.

In the sections that follow I begin by describing the context for my current research into leadership for capacity building in early childhood services. This work uses principles of cultural-historical activity theory (CHAT) to develop leaders who know how to work systemically and systematically to build centre cultures anchored in ethical, high-quality practices. I illustrate my argument with an example from recent work in Melbourne, Australia, where contradictions arose between centre leaders and their employing authority in relation to an apparently minor issue. This example serves to show how even the most everyday issues facing centre leaders offer opportunities for their teams to advocate for children and families.

## The educational leader in Australian early childhood education and care settings

In the Australian context, early childhood education and care services are required to designate an 'Educational Leader' who is responsible for leading curriculum implementation in their centre. The emphasis of this position is on leading learning, both for children through the *Early Years Learning Framework* (Department of Education, Employment and Workplace Relations, 2009) and for colleagues through localised professional development activities. This initiative has seen the flourishing of mentoring programmes to support these Educational Leaders, both through the mentoring *of* leaders and by developing leaders *as* mentors of their colleagues.

However, approaches such as mentoring may not be culturally suited to early childhood services if they are all based on one-to-one models of professional development. Coaching and mentoring approaches often privilege a cultural world view predicated on the centrality of the individual rather than the community. This approach has implications for the usefulness of mentoring models in indigenous and other communities, where the development of the collective is understood as preceding individual growth, not vice versa. Such models are also easily confounded by high staff turnover and limited resources of time and money to support non-contact activities.

## Developing the capacity of leaders to develop centres as systems

Given the complexity and responsibility involved in leadership in early childhood services, I argue for an approach to the development of leadership capacity that goes beyond understanding leadership as a set of specific skills and dispositions that inhere in individuals; an approach that goes beyond coaching and mentoring individuals appointed as Educational Leaders. The orientation I propose can require a profound shift in the thinking of leaders: from seeing themselves and their colleagues as individuals to be shaped one by one, to seeing their teams as co-participants in distinctive cultural practices. The work of leadership shifts from 'How can I get others to change?' to 'How can we work together to change our centre's norms of practice?' I argue that it is the shifting of these norms, rather than changing individual dispositions and capacities, that will keep the field moving towards ethical outcomes that strengthen the human dignity of children, their families and colleagues.

In my work in Melbourne with 11 centres (Nuttall, Thomas, & Wood, 2014) I have been exploring an approach to leadership development that employs a research and development methodology known as developmental work research (DWR) (Engeström, 2005; Nuttall, 2013). This approach provides Educational Leaders with conceptual tools they can use to bring norms of centre practice to conscious awareness in relation to key concepts drawn from cultural-historical activity theory: 'rules', 'cultural tools', 'division of labour' and 'objects of activity'. In our collaborations we explore questions such as:

- What are the explicit and implicit *rules* in the centre for how people should think and behave?
- How does the group organise itself (the *division of labour*) to ensure everything that needs to be done gets done?
- What are the important artefacts and conceptual *tools* the group uses to mediate important tasks (e.g. children's assessment portfolios, staff rosters, copies of curriculum frameworks, etc.)?

The most important question, however, relates to the *object of activity*: what is the group working on? This is not a trivial question. Practices in collaborative workplaces such as early childhood centres involve carrying out tasks that are characteristic of what the group is trying to achieve. In early childhood services these tasks are frequently routine and time limited, such as mealtimes. They can also be subtler and irregular, such as engaging in extended conversations with children or observing each other's practice as a form of peer coaching. Either way, every task is mediated by cultural understanding about who does it (the division of labour), the rules that apply to how it's done, and the use of cultural tools (in the form of resources or concepts) to get the job done. Enculturation into norms of practice is a process of internalising these norms to the point where educators can act on them seamlessly throughout the working day.

A second component of a DWR approach is the exploration of the *contradictions* that inevitably arise within collective practice. By contradictions I do not mean interpersonal conflict or differences in teaching philosophy or style (although these can and do occur). Rather, contradictions relate to the structural tensions that arise from misalignments within or between the rules, the cultural tools available to the participants, and the division of labour. A simple leadership example might be tension between an explicit rule—that staff members are welcome to contribute to the agenda of the staff meeting—and how the agenda actually gets written, as when the leader circulates their own pre-populated meeting agenda in advance of staff meetings. Until the contradiction between the official (explicit) rule and the actual (implicit) rule is consciously explored, the leader may continue to puzzle over why staff members seem reluctant to contribute to the staff meeting agenda.

Within a DWR approach, participants begin by identifying an object of activity in their work and the persistent structural tensions or contradictions they think are confounding achievement of this object in their centre. Having identified a contradiction they want to address, they work with their teams to adapt local rules, tools and/or divisions of labour to resolve the contradiction and to develop a richer, "expanded" (Engeström, 2001) understanding of the workplace object. A leader seeking genuine input from staff into the meeting agenda could, for example, invite educators to note suggested agenda items on a whiteboard in the staffroom in advance of the meeting. Each meeting could then begin by negotiating the priority order of these items.

This example may seem banal and the solution rather obvious (and by no means the only solution), but anyone who has worked in a large, busy early childhood centre will relate to the ways in which apparently modest changes in leadership practices can dramatically influence cultural norms of inclusion, democratic participation and morale. In this example, a simple change in leadership practice can point to an expanded understanding of key workplace concepts and practices such as agency, collaboration and professional contribution. By bringing to the surface problematic cultural practices and thinking creatively about solutions, a DWR approach seeks to bring everyday practices into stronger and richer alignment with centres' longer-term aspirations.

## *An example of advocacy enacted through leaders bringing contradictions to consciousness*

As DWR participants work to identify contradictions they wish to resolve in their work, they inevitably begin to spot contradictions that are the result of expectations imposed by systems beyond their immediate centre system. These may be macro-level systems, such as government (encountered through policy or regulations), or smaller-scale systems such as individual families. The following example shows how contradictions can arise at the point where all three of these systems meet: families, centres and external governance (in this case, a local government body operating multiple early childhood services). Another reason for sharing this example is to show how a group of educational leaders used a DWR analysis to respond as advocates for children. The example is presented as a composite narrative (Goodley, Lawthom, Clough, & Moore, 2004), drawn from interviews and workshop discussions with four of the educational leaders in the project.

### Breakfast at home *versus* breakfast at the centre

Educators in four of the centres participating in the developmental work research (DWR) project had noticed increasing numbers of children arriving in the morning who had not eaten breakfast. The centres did not provide breakfast as part of their service so the parents were bringing boxes of cereal for educators to serve. Initially this was not a problem, but as the practice grew the centres were finding they didn't have sufficient space to store the breakfast foods. The local government authority that held the licence for the centres and employed the educators suggested that the Educational Leaders (in this case they were also the centre directors) tell the parents that the children must eat breakfast before they arrived in the morning. The authority was concerned risks would arise around storage and food-handling issues.

The directors were not happy with this advice. They recognised the parents were trying to get their children to the centre as well as get to work on time, and the directors felt they should support these busy parents at the start of the day. Initially the directors felt this was a problem they had to resolve individually, centre by centre. However, by using the DWR methodology they were able to identify contradictions that were interfering with an important object of activity: supporting families. They understood the perspective of the employer that food safety was essential (a rule) but felt that they had not been offered the creative solution they needed.

The directors decided to meet with the employing authority to bring to conscious awareness the contradiction that had arisen between the object of supporting parents and the rule of forbidding parents to bring children's breakfasts to the centre. Shona (not her real name), one of the directors, described how the methodology helped her make the shift from seeing the situation as a problem for her to solve alone, to one of distributed responsibility—and therefore greatly enhanced problem-solving potential—across the neighbouring systems of centre, families and the employing authority:

> [The methodology] has helped from really small, tiny, little conversations we've been having centre-based to the current one at the moment, about the whole breakfast thing, and that's more of a network [issue]. So there's a couple of us that are actually jumping on board with this and taking that step further to higher [city] management and going, "Well, this is what you want, but how are we going to achieve it?" ... having this tool [the model explored during the research] has given me the confidence to actually go, "No, this is what I'm seeing and can I get some help with it?" It's not just about me always having the answers and saying "Yes, it's what I've said, what are you going to do for me and how are we going to achieve this outcome if we've got different rules?"

In this example we see several Educational Leaders coming together to work on the boundaries where multiple systems overlap: the system of the centre; the system of the employing authority; and the systems of centre families. Each of these systems is working on the same important task—responding to the demands facing centre families—but each is working on it in ways that give rise to structural tensions between the three systems. Shona realised that the three systems were applying different expectations about who does what and why: the families were working on getting to the centre and work on time, the employer was working on minimising risk, and the teachers wanted the children to have a breakfast that would see them through the day. By being able to think about the situation at the level of systems, Shona realised she did not have to solve this misalignment on her own, and that the situation could not be resolved by movement within just one system: all three systems would need to adapt aspects of their practice. Although this example happened to involve multiple Educational Leaders focused on the same object, the project contained many more examples of individual Educational Leaders making change at the level of their own centre system.

## *Advocacy for social change in early childhood education*

This way of thinking about structural tensions understands misalignment as a positive force, since examining structural tensions in a systematic way brings them safely to the surface and treats them as a source of productive dialogue, not as a source of stress and insecurity. Shona and her colleagues were learning to think about their centres as places where people come together to engage in distinctive and negotiated cultural practices, rather than as places where teachers make individual and sometimes idiosyncratic decisions about practice. In strategising to make the morning routine easier for centre families, Shona and her colleagues provide an example of how everyday practices can enact advocacy for children and families just as much as the grand gestures of fundraising, social media campaigns and political action.

However, Shona and her colleagues not only had to engage with the adjacent objects, rules, tools and divisions of labour of local government authority, but also had to bring the norms of practice in their individual centre systems into alignment with the object of supporting families. In each of the four centres there were educators who challenged their centre director, arguing that it was not the responsibility of staff to serve breakfast to the children. Part of the work of advocacy for leaders in education is to establish and maintain the cultural norms of education institutions, and effective leaders in early childhood education not only act as advocates but build the capacity of others to view early childhood education as a site for change. By working with their colleagues in ways that focused on desired objects and outcomes, rather than meeting the preferences of individual staff, these directors were able to increase the capacity of their teams to orient themselves more strongly toward families' and children's needs.

The need for approaches to leadership development that support leaders to think and work systemically is pressing in early childhood education and care internationally; the field has not been constructed culturally, professionally or industrially to achieve long-term development by focusing solely at the level of individual workers. The capacity to think about centres as culturally distinctive systems that interact with other social systems, such as health, justice and welfare, is increasingly important for leaders in early childhood services. This capacity begins with being able to work through problems of practice by responding to contradictions within immediate centre systems. Without this capacity, the profession lacks the conceptual tools to engage with the deep contradictions that hinder society's capacity to ensure every child is healthy, safe and protected.

## *References*

Department of Education, Employment and Workplace Relations. (2009). *Belonging, being & becoming: The early years learning framework for Australia*. Canberra, ACT, Australia: Department of Education, Employment and Workplace Relations.

Engeström, Y. (2001). Expansive learning at work: Toward an activity theoretical reconceptualization. *Journal of Education and Work, 14*(1), 133–156.

Engeström, Y. (2005). *Developmental work research: Expanding activity theory in practice*. Berlin, Germany: Lehmanns Media.

Goodley, D., Lawthom, R., Clough, P., & Moore, M. (2004). *Researching life stories: Method, theory and analyses in a biographical age*. London, UK: RoutledgeFalmer.

Nuttall, J. (2013). The potential of Developmental Work Research as a professional learning methodology in early childhood education. *Contemporary Issues in Early Childhood, 3*, 201–211.

Nuttall, J., Thomas, L., & Wood, E. (2014). Travelling policy reforms re-configuring the work of early childhood educators in Australia. *Globalisation, Societies and Education, 12*(3), 358–372.

# Chapter 9 The Swedish preschool system in transition

Ingrid Pramling Samuelsson and Pia Williams

## *Introduction*

In Sweden, participation in preschools that offer the child a good start to school and life is seen as an aspect of every child's right to education. This chapter explores how this goal of an equal right to attend preschool from the age of 1 year is playing out in a changing societal context, and how preschool in Sweden meets the needs of today's children and families. It describes the changes and the contemporary situation when the large majority of children attend preschool from their early years.

## *Research context*

Recent years have seen a paradigm shift in pedagogical approaches to foster children's learning and development based on Vygotsky's theories (1986, 1998). Research has confirmed that children learn through relationships with parents, preschool staff, other adults and peers (e.g. Løkken, 2000; Sommer, 2012; Williams, Sheridan, & Sandberg, 2014). The best conditions for learning in educational environments occur when children have opportunities to participate in programmes with engaged, experienced, professional teachers, and where interactions between them facilitate knowledge building and skills and attitudes (Sheridan, Williams, & Pramling Samuelsson, 2014; Siraj-Blatchford, 2010). This is now supported by two decades of socio-cognition research. Iram Siraj-Blatchford argues that children's cognitive and social learning are of equal importance. Both of these are apparent in the Swedish preschool curriculum (Swedish National Agency for Education, 1998/2010). Collaborating with others is a way of practising and developing democratic understanding, and democratic values are deemed fundamental in the Swedish preschool curriculum.

Focusing on the youngest children in a society has also been found to be socioeconomically profitable and of great importance, not least for public health (Heckman, 2006). Most effective for the individual, family and society are investments in children 1 to 3 years old (Britto & Ulkuer, 2012).

## *Forty years of statutory preschool*

Driven by strong women, preschool has a long tradition in Sweden of providing for older preschool children. In the middle of the 1960s women entering the labour market demanded daycare for children (Klinth & Johansson, 2010). In response, the government asked a delegation to examine expanding care and education for young children (SOU, 1972, p. 26). The result was a new law in 1975 that offered 1 year of free preschool for children aged 5 and 6 years. The delegation also recommended integrating *daycare* and *kindergarten* into a united preschool system, with a curriculum, trained preschool teachers, and activities based on modern theories of child development and learning. The Swedish National Agency for Education, responsible for schools, became responsible for administering preschools at the national level.

After free attendance at preschool for 6-year-olds was granted, parents sought government-funded preschooling for younger children. However, achieving the right of all children from 1 year of age to participate in preschool has been a long and winding path, although the Swedish government and the labour market had a clear intention to move in this direction (Regeringskansliet, 2015). Expansion of provision for younger preschoolers contributed to a child-centred approach in preschool, where play, learning and care are strongly integrated. Parents were pleased with preschool, which is why very few considered letting their children begin school at 6 years of age, even though school start policy became flexible and it was possible to start before the age of 7. In the 1990s Sweden began offering preschool classes in schools for 6-year-olds. About the same time, all parents gained the right to a place for their child in preschool within a few months of the time they requested it.

## *The situation today*

Since 2003, 3 hours a day of free preschool is provided for children aged 3 years and older whose parents want it. The Swedish government now spends 1.3 percent of the country's Gross Domestic Product (GDP) on preschool annually (European Commission, 2014), and preschool is heavily subsidised by the government. The maximum fee policy for full-day preschool (in Swedish, "max-taxa") provides equity of access to children: it is designed to not hinder access to preschool. Currently the maximum fee is around €140 per month for the first child, and then a decreasing sum for each additional child in the family.

Increasingly, preschool is seen as an aspect of each child's right to a good start in life. Today most parents choose preschool and are satisfied with it. In 2013 more than 470,000 children were enrolled, with almost 96 percent of all children aged 3 to 5 years attending preschool. A survey of parents of 124,000 children by the Swedish National Agency for Education (2013) revealed that 90 percent felt that the staff did a good job, their children were safe and the preschool pedagogy met their expectations. Internationally, Swedish preschools have historically been highly regarded.

More than 50 percent of all children enrolled in preschool are 3 years old or younger. A high number of children in preschool speak a language other than Swedish, since by 2015 Sweden had accepted more immigrants than any other European country relative to the size of its population.

## Swedish international rankings

Early this century the Swedish preschool system topped the OECD[1] rankings for early childhood education. International comparison measurements are generally concerned with what society does for children and families (Williams, Sheridan, & Pramling Samuelsson, 2016). Indicators include paid parental leave, access to places, funding support from the government, subsidised fees, trained preschool personnel (at least one adult per 15 children), at least 1 percent of the GDP transferred to childcare, and child poverty being lower than 10 percent of children in the country (Lien Foundation, 2012; UNICEF, 2008).

However, recently the OECD (2015) reported that Sweden's international ranking has declined from first to third place. Expansion of preschool places, decentralisation of their administration to municipalities, changes in the population profile through immigration and some changes in policy appear to be contributing factors to growing inequality and a decrease in the quality of Swedish early education.

The policy changes noticed by both teachers and parents were group size and child and parent participation in the curriculum. Research with teachers as participants has shone a light on pedagogical challenges associated with larger groups, increased parent participation and changes associated with the revised curriculum. The existing workforce simply hasn't had adequate training and professional development to be comfortable with implementing the pedagogical changes needed.

## Inequality

Data from the National Supervisory Authority's evaluation of preschool showed an increase in inequality: specifically, the staff:children ratio, the level of teacher training and group sizes are worse where families have poor social and economic conditions, and these variables affect children's wellbeing, learning and development. Children's rights to a good and equal start in life have deteriorated (Göteborgs Stad, 2005, 2014; Malmö stad, 2014; Swedish School Inspectorate, 2012, 2016).

The statistics on the deployment of qualified teachers in municipalities reveal two types of inequality. These issues of inequality, which need to be addressed at the political level as well as at the local level

---

1 Organisation for Economic Cooperation and Development.

of the preschool, are that groups where over 30 percent of the children are migrants who speak a language other than Swedish have an average of 47 percent qualified preschool teachers; municipalities with fewer than 5 percent of migrant children on their preschool rolls have an average of 61 percent of their staff with teaching qualifications. Put simply, where there are more children with a mother tongue other than Swedish, there are fewer qualified teachers on the staff.

Second, a similar imbalance occurs in toddler groups (with a maximum of 13 children, i.e. small groups), in larger-sized groups where an average of 34 percent of the staff are qualified, while in smaller-sized groups the average is 51 percent. These data show that children who most need closer relationships, and to relate to adults who have a conscious approach to interaction and communication, have less access to qualified teachers.

## Group size

Group sizes have increased as enrolments have risen, such that almost all children participate. Parents today are conscious of the need for high-quality preschools with trained preschool teachers. There are numerous articles in the media in which parents and preschool staff make their voices heard concerning quality, especially in relation to group size. They say there are too many children in each group (as reported in a survey by Pramling, Samuelsson, Sheridan, Williams, & Nasiopoulou, 2014). Statistics from the Swedish National Agency for Education (2015) show a national average of 16.7 children per group (with a range between municipalities of 11 to 26 children per group). The ratio is 5.2 children per adult across all ages.

Williams, Sheridan and Pramling Samuelsson (2016) surveyed 698 preschool teachers to obtain their views on group size in preschool. The teachers raised a number of issues, which included the number of children in a group, the composition of groups (age, special needs, children with another mother tongue), communication, teacher competence, and the environment and facilities. In the study (Williams et al., 2016), the preschool teachers answered a questionnaire that was broadly about children's opportunities to learn related to group size. One of the questions concerned children's participation in preschool. Teachers said it is more difficult to let children participate and influence everyday activities when there are "too many children in the group". Many teachers described their day as highly structured and organised to maintain order in larger groups.

## *Children's and parents' rights to participation*

In most descriptions of the features of quality in preschool, co-operation with parents is a key factor (Sheridan, 2009). In the Swedish curriculum both parents' and children's rights are referred to. The curriculum states that the teacher is responsible for giving parents the opportunity to exercise influence in preschool regarding content, and for involving parents in assessing the preschool's work (Swedish National Agency for Education, 1998/2010). A European study (Pramling Samuelsson & Cojocaru, 2016) showed that Sweden is different from most European countries in giving parents this right to influence what goes on in preschool.

How parents exercise their right to participate and influence varies greatly between different preschools. It has been challenging for teachers, not least when working with parents from different cultures, which is common in the preschool system today when every fifth child has a different mother tongue to Swedish (Swedish National Agency for Education, 2013). Immigrant parents want their children to fit into the customs of preschool, yet they have different views on both pedagogy and democracy. They tend to focus on issues of language (Kultti & Pramling Samuelsson, 2016; Vandenbroeck, 2007). Tobin, Arzubiaga and Adair (2013) report that immigrant parents often want their children to learn to read and write early in preschool, while Swedish parents typically want their children to make friends and play.

The influence of the child is referred to in the curriculum (Swedish National Agency for Education, 1998/2010). The curriculum gives three goals the preschool should ensure for each child:

- she/he develops the ability to express his/her thoughts and views, and thus has the opportunity to influence his/her own situation
- she/he develops the ability to accept responsibility for his/her own actions and the preschool's environment
- she/he develops the ability to understand and act in accordance with democratic principles by participating in different kinds of co-operation and decision making (p. 12).

Our study (Williams et al., 2016) has shown that teachers' support for children's participation varies. Children and adults may work for part of the day in smaller groups, often based on the children's age, where there are fewer possibilities for the children to make choices. Teachers also described strategies for listening more to the children and being sensitive to their wishes, but some admitted that although they listened, they also indirectly steered the children to do what the teachers wanted.

Teachers claimed that the children participate and have an influence on their own play, since play involves the children's own choices. However, there is a spectrum of choice possibilities. On the one hand there is a commonly used system of 'cards for choice'. This involves cards representing various areas of the classroom, and the children choose a card related to what they want to do or play with for a designated period of time. In reality, the teachers can manipulate choice by deciding who makes the first choice, how many children can choose a specific activity, how the group of children is organised, and so on. These practices raise questions about how great the choice is for children, and to what extent they can influence what goes on in preschool.

On the other hand, some teachers allow children to decide both what they want to do and what content they are going to work with. The viewpoint of these teachers seems to be that everything has to start from each child's experience and interest. Another system of choice involves teachers asking children to vote: they lay out various choices in front of children and ask them to take a stand on which of the options they want. What the majority of the children choose is what everyone does.

## *Pedagogical challenges for preschool teachers*

Many of the teachers are experiencing challenges related to the revised curriculum (Swedish National Agency for Education, 2010), with its additional responsibilities for documentation, evaluation and developing practice. Goals for language and communication, mathematics, natural science and technology learning areas have been amplified.

Preschool teachers are now designated as leaders of each team,[2] with the main responsibility for children's learning, development and care. Earlier the whole team had this responsibility. These changed requirements are clearly evident in the content of preschool teacher education. However, many preschool teachers who have many years of experience feel unsure about what the recent changes mean.

Our research (Pramling Samuelsson, Williams, & Sheridan, 2015; Sheridan et al., 2014; Williams et al., 2016) revealed that preschool teachers endorse individualised learning. This sometimes leads to the importance of collaboration and peer learning being overshadowed. The teachers feel stressed about individualisation when they cannot find time to meet and communicate with each child every day, and this contributes to their perception that the groups are too large.

One of the greatest challenges for preschool staff is to develop pedagogy to be more content-oriented yet keep the social and play dimensions central. This means strengthening the preschool didactic approach, in which play and learning are integrated (Pramling Samuelsson & Asplund Carlsson, 2008). It is also important that teachers implement an experience-oriented theory (Pramling Samuelsson & Pramling, 2016; Siraj-Blatchford, 2010; Sheridan, Sandberg, & Williams, 2015), whereby communication and interactions between children and teachers, and between peers, is central to children's learning.

Last, but not least, the profession has to *meet* the challenge of the notion of teaching, which is new in Swedish preschool (Doverborg, Pramling & Pramling Samuelsson, 2013; Jonsson, Williams, & Pramling Samuelsson, submitted). Traditionally, teaching has been associated with compulsory school education and now has to be reinterpreted for the education of young children. This positions the participation of the teacher in children's learning and play as central (Løndal & Greve, 2015).

## *Concluding comments*

Swedish preschool has been undergoing an expansive period, with associated policy changes. Most children are enrolled in preschool, and

---

2  A team is usually made up of three adults, with possible team combinations being: two university-educated teachers and one nursery nurse; two nursery nurses and one teacher; or three university-educated teachers.

families expect high-quality early childhood education and care practices. The UN's proposed Sustainable Development Goals (2015) state that every child should be assured of an inclusive and equitable quality education, promoting lifelong learning opportunities. Society and preschool education intertwine in order to provide all children with the opportunity for an equal start in life in a preschool of high quality. According to the Education Act (SFS 2010:800), equality is highlighted in three fundamental aspects: equal access to education, equal quality of education, and the principle that education should be *compensatory*.

Preschool has unique opportunities to compensate for unequal social conditions by providing high-quality conditions for learning, development and wellbeing (Persson, 2010, 2015). In a high-quality preschool, competent teachers adapt environments, content and activities to children's diverse backgrounds, experiences and culture (Sheridan & Williams, 2016). Equity means that all children encounter competent and dedicated preschool teachers in a stimulating, learning environment where they can learn and develop their potential. Thus, democracy, equality and equity in preschool depend on the teachers' competence as they communicate, interact, understand and listen to the children. In these types of settings, children feel involved and able to participate in their learning processes.

## References

Britto, P., & Ulkuer, U. (2012). Child development in developing countries: Child rights and policy implications. *Child Development, 83*(1), 92–103.

Doverborg, E., Pramling, N., & Pramling Samuelsson, I. (2013). *Att undervisa barn i förskolan*. [To teach in preschool]. Stockholm, Sweden: Liber.

European Commission, EACEA, Eurydike, & Eurostat. (2014). *Key data on early childhood education and care in Europe* (2014 ed.). Eurydice and Eurostat Report. Luxembourg: Publications Office of the European Union.

Göteborgs Stad. (2005). *Storstad: Om storstadssatsningen i Göteborg*. [Large City: About funding in Gothenburg]. Göteborg, Sweden: Elanders.

Göteborgs Stad. (2014). *Skillnader I livsvillkor och hälsa i Göteborg: Hela staden social hållbar*. [Differences in living and health in Gothenburg]. https://goteborg.se/wps/wcm/connect/34c40e2c-2fea-4867-954a-4a6f022fe505/Skillnader-i-livsvillkor-och-h%C3%A4lsa-2014-Huvudrapport1.pdf?MOD=AJPERES

Heckman, J. (2006). Skill formation and the economics of investing in disadvantaged children. *Science, 312*(5782), 1900–1902.

Jonsson, A., Williams, P., & Pramling Samuelsson, I. (submitted). Undervisningsbegreppet och dess innebörder uttryckta av förskolans lärare. [Teaching in preschool]

Klinth, R., & Johansson, T. (2010). *Nya svenska fäder.* [New Swedish fathers]. Umeå, Sweden: Borea.

Kultti, A., & Pramling Samuelsson, I. (2016). Investing in home-preschool collaboration for understanding social worlds of multilingual children. *Journal of Early Childhood Education Research, 5*(1), 69–91. Retrieved from http://jecer.org/fi.

Lien Foundation. (2012). *Starting well: Benchmarking early education across the world.* A report from the Economist Intelligence Unit, commissioned by Lien Foundation. Singapore: Lien Foundation.

Løkken, G. (2000). *Toddler peer culture: The social style of one and two year old body-subjects in everyday interaction.* Trondheim, Norway: Pedagogisk institutt, Fakultet for samfunnsvitenskap og teknologiledelse, Norges teknisk-naturvitenskapelige universitet.

Løndal, K., & Greve, A. (2015). Didactic approaches to child-managed play: Analyses of teachers' interaction styles in kindergartens and after-school programmes in Norway. *International Journal of Early Childhood, 47*: 461–479.

Malmö stad. (2014). *Malmös väg mot en hållbar framtid: Hälsa, välfärd och rättvisa* (Report). [Malmö's path towards a sustainable future]. Malmö, Sweden: Kommissionen för ett socialt hållbart. Retrieved from http://malmo.se/download/ 18.3108a6ec1445513e589b90/1393252127222/malmoprocentCCprocent88kommissionen_slutrapport_2014.pdf

OECD. (2015). *Education at a glance: OECD indicators: Better policies for better life.* Paris, France: OECD. Retrieved from http://www.oecdilibrary.org/docserver/download/9615031e.pdf?expires=1461830458&id=id&accname=guest&checksum=5C2A9EE6A96EA26F4532EF5820CA9CB7

Persson, S. (2010). *Perspektiv på barndom och barns lärande: En kunskapsöversikt om lärande i förskolan och grundskolans tidigare år.* [Perspective on childhood and children's learning: An overview about learning in preschool and primary school]. Stockholm, Sweden: Fritzes.

Persson, S. (2015). *En likvärdig förskola för alla barn: Innebörder och indikatorer.*

[An equal preschool for all: Meaning and indicators]. Vetenskapsrådets rapportserie. Stockholm, Sweden: Vetenskapsrådet.

Pramling Samuelsson, I., & Asplund Carlsson, M. (2008). The playing learning child: Towards a pedagogy of early childhood. *Scandinavian Journal of Educational Research, 52*(6), 623–641.

Pramling Samuelsson, I., & Cojocaru, S. (2016). Diverse perspectives of participation in Denmark, Greece, Germany, Hungary, Iceland, Romania and Sweden. In K. Fisher, I. Kaschefi-Haude, & J. Schneider (Eds.), *Strengthen activity-oriented interaction and growth in the early years and transition: Voices of participation.* 538783-LLP-1-2013-1-DE-Comenius-CMP. Retrieved from http://www.signals-eu.com/.

Pramling Samuelsson, I., & Pramling, N. (2016). Variation theory of learning and developmental pedagogy: Two context-related models of learning grounded in phenomenography. *Scandinavian Journal of Educational Research. 60*(3). http://dx.doi.org/10.1080/00313831.2015.1120232

Pramling Samuelsson, I., Sheridan, S., Williams, P., & Nasiopoulou, P. (2014). Stora barngrupper i förskolan – ett medieperspektiv. In J. Balldin, J. Dahlbeck, A. Harju, & P. Lilja (Eds.), *Om förskolan och de yngre barnen: Historiska och nutida nedslag* [Large child groups in preschool in a media perspective]. (pp. 101–114). Lund, Sweden: Studentlitteratur.

Pramling Samuelsson, I., Williams, P., & Sheridan, S. (2015). Stora barngrupper i förskolan relaterat till läroplanens intentioner. *Nordic Early Childhood Education Research Journal, 9*(7), 1-14. [Large child groups in preschool related to the intention of the curriculum]

Regeringskansliet (2015, 18 November). *1975-2015 40 år med lagstadgad förskola.* [40 years with statutory preschool]. Seminarium anordnad i Riksdagens andrakammare.

SFS. (2010:800). *Skollag.* . [Swedish Education Act]. Stockholm, Sweden: Utbildningsdepartementet.

Sheridan, S. (2009). Discerning pedagogical quality in preschool. *Scandinavian Journal of Educational Research, 53*(3), 245–261.

Sheridan, S., Sandberg, A., & Williams, P. (2015). *Förskollärarkompetens i förändring.* [Preschool teacher competence in change]. Lund, Sweden: Studentlitteratur.

Sheridan, S., & Williams, P. (2016). *Barngruppers storlek i förskolan. En kartläggning av aktuell pedagogisk, utvecklingspsykologisk och socialpsykologisk forskning.* [The size of the groups in preschool: An overview of pedagogical, development and social psychological research]. Stockholm, Sweden: Skolverket.

Sheridan, S., Williams, P., & Pramling Samuelsson, I. (2014). Group size and organizational conditions for children's learning in preschool: A teacher perspective. *Educational Research, 56*(4), 379–397.

Siraj-Blatchford, I. (2010). A focus on pedagogy: Case studies of effective practice. In K. Sylva, E. Melhuish, P. Sammons, I. Siraj-Blatchford, & B. Taggart (Eds.), *Early childhood matters: Evidence from the Effective Preschool and Primary Education Project* (pp. 149–165). London, UK: Routledge.

Sommer, D. (2012). *A childhood psychology: Young children in changing times.* Basingstoke, UK: Palgrave Macmillan.

SOU. (1972:26). *Förskolan I: Betänkande utgivet av Barnstugeutredningen.* [Preschool] Stockholm, Sweden: Fritzes

Swedish National Agency for Education. (1998/2016). *Curriculum for preschool, Lpfö98.* Revised in 2016. Stockholm, Sweden: Skolverket.

Swedish National Agency for Education. (2013). *Beskrivande data 2013: Förskola, skola och vuxenutbildning.* [Descriptive data]. Skolverkets rapport nr 399. Stockholm, Sweden: Skolverket.

Swedish National Agency for Education. (2015). *Beskrivande data 2015.* Retrieved from http://www.skolverket.se/statistik-och-utvardering/statistik-i-tabeller/forskola.

Swedish School Inspectorate. (2012). *Förskola, före skola: Lärande och bärande: Kvalitetsgranskningsrapport om förskolans arbete med det förstärkta pedagogiska uppdraget.* [Preschool, before school. Learning and bearing: quality review report on preschool work with strengthened educational mission]. Stockholm, Sweden: Skolinspektionen.

Swedish School Inspectorate. (2016). *Trygghet och lärande för barn under 3år: En ögonblicksbild av förskolans vardag.* [Security and learning for children under 3 years of age: A snapshot of every-day life in preschool]. Stockholm, Sweden: Skolinspektionen.

Tobin, J., Arzubiaga, A., & Adair, J. K. (2013). *Children crossing borders: Immigrant parent and teacher perspectives on preschool.* New York, NY: Russell Sage.

UNICEF. (2008). *The child care transition: A league table of early childhood education and care in economically advanced countries.* Florence, Italy: UNICEF Innocenti Research Centre.

Vandenbroeck, M. (2007). Beyond anti-bias education: Changing conceptions of diversity and equity in European early childhood education. *European Early Childhood Education Research Journal*, 15(1), 21–35.

Vygotsky, L. S. (1986 [1934]). *Thought and language.* Cambridge, MA: MIT Press.

Vygotsky, L. S. (1998). *The collected works of L. S. Vygotsky. Volume 5: Child psychology.* New York, NY: Plenum.

Williams, P., Sheridan, S., & Pramling Samuelsson, I. (2016). *Barngruppens storlek i förskolan: Konsekvenser för utveckling och kvalitet.* [Group size in preschool: Consequences for development and quality]. Stockholm, Sweden: Natur & Kultur.

Williams, P., Sheridan, S., & Sandberg, A. (2014). Preschool: An arena for children's learning of social and cognitive knowledge. *Early Years, 34*(3), 226–240.

# Chapter 10 Towards a holistic approach to early childhood education

Peter Moss

I remember going to a seminar in London in the 1990s to hear about changes afoot in early childhood services in New Zealand. Her account of things seemed remarkable, an initial impression confirmed subsequently from various sources, including my own visits. What emerged was a country making serious attempts to break the mould, to turn away from the path followed by other Anglophone countries with its defining features of a split system, under-investment, and reliance on a poorly qualified, low-paid female workforce to keep the whole rickety edifice (literally) in business. Here, instead, was a serious attempt to develop an integrated early childhood system, at the heart of which was a well-qualified workforce engaging with innovative approaches to curriculum, evaluation and research, and a holistic approach to working with children and families based on a concept of education in its broadest sense.

What I want to do in this chapter is explore further the concept of an integrated early childhood system, in particular considering why it matters, what it means and how far it has been achieved in Europe and, across the other side of the world, in New Zealand. I want to suggest that New Zealand, though some way off achieving full integration, has made some large strides towards this goal during a reform process initiated in 1988 by the publication of *Education to Be More* (Department of Education, 1988), the report of a government-established Early Childhood Care and Education Working Group. Last, but not least, I want to salute the contribution to this impressive achievement of a group of exceptional women, whose clear vision and determined application have played such an important and sustained part in propelling and defending the reform process—a group including Anne Smith.

## From split to integrated systems of early childhood

Early childhood services in every country have divided origins, often going back to the 19th century: 'daycare' services, usually for poorer families and serving a welfare role of childcare for working parents and preventive work with 'problem' families; and education or kindergarten services, in many cases originally for middle-class families and offering play or education provision. While the former typically provided full-day provision for children under (and sometimes over) 3 years of age, the latter were mainly confined to part-time provision for children aged over 3 years. Further sectoral differences covered funding, type of provision, overseeing ministry and workforce.

Such split systems are a legacy in many countries, despite being the subject of critical discussion since the 1970s (Kahn & Kamerman, 1976; OECD, 1974) highlighting issues of fragmentation, divisiveness, inequality and discontinuity. A 2010 report from UNESCO observed that

> analyses have identified several core problems. For example, education is considered to begin when children are aged 3 or 4, with younger children defined as needing only minding or care while their parents work. Governments assume greater responsibility for education for children over three years, thus investing more public funding in early education than in childcare services for younger children. Differences between services in welfare and education in key areas such as access, regulation, funding and workforce, lead to problems of inequality and lack of continuity for children, parents and workers. (Kaga, Bennett, & Moss, 2010, p. 7)

That report sought to go further by identifying the criteria for defining early childhood systems that had moved from being split to fully integrated. Seven criteria were put forward, six of which could be defined as structural: policy making and administration; access to services; funding (including what parents pay); regulation (including curriculum or similar guidelines); workforce (including structure, education and pay); and type of provision. Today I would qualify two of these. Curriculum, I think, can be considered a separate criterion in those cases where it is not prescriptive and detailed, but instead operates as a broad pedagogical framework allowing for local interpretation and addition; in other words, downplaying regulation in favour of diversity and experimentation. Type of provision, if it is to count towards a fully integrated system, can include some diversity of provision (in terms of age groups covered or management auspices), but must consist of provision that is open to all children, irrespective of parental income, employment or other characteristics; for instance, a service where some types of provision (such as day nurseries in England) are only for children of employed parents should not count as fully integrated.

The seventh criterion is both the least tangible and, in some ways, the most important, being conceptual. The UNESCO report put it like this:

> Important as structural areas are for defining integration, equally important is conceptual integration. To what extent does the whole ECCE system share an understanding of what it is for and what it is doing, and how far is this expressed in a common language? In short, has the system got beyond thinking and talking about 'childcare' and 'education'? Of course, thinking and talking need not convert into policy and practice, so we might best consider this as a necessary but not sufficient condition for deep integration of the whole system.
> (Kaga et al., p. 28)

Conceptual integration is about a holistic idea of early childhood provision and a holistic view of the child; or, put another way, the impossibility of imagining that education, care and upbringing could ever be separated out. This holistic perspective is, for example, embedded in the fully integrated Swedish system and expressed in the (framework) Swedish Preschool Curriculum, which describes the task of the preschool in the following inclusive terms:

The preschool should lay the foundations for lifelong learning.
The preschool should be enjoyable, secure, and rich in learning for all children. The preschool should stimulate children's development and learning and offer secure care. Activities should be based on a holistic view of the child and his or her needs and be designed so that care, socialisation and learning together form a coherent whole. (Skolverket, 2010, p.4)

## Integration in Europe and New Zealand

I turn now to look at whether and how far fully integrated early childhood systems have been achieved in Europe, by which I mean the 28 member states of the European Union (EU), including for the moment the United Kingdom, plus three other countries in Europe but not in the EU: Iceland, Norway and Switzerland. Of these 31 countries, six (the five Nordic states and Slovenia) are fully integrated. Sweden illustrates what this means in practice. I have already referred to the country's conceptual integration, but this is complemented by full structural integration: the system is seamless, with no sign left of the country's historical split between nurseries providing care and kindergartens providing education. There is now a universal entitlement for all children to attend services from 12 months of age (after the end of well-paid parental leave), an entitlement not just on paper but implemented in practice. The great majority of children go to one type of provision, the preschool, a centre that takes children from 1 to 6 years and is staffed by graduate preschool teachers and qualified assistants (roughly in the ratio of 50:50), both specialising in work with the whole of this preschool age group. There is a common funding framework, with 525 hours per year of free attendance for 4- and 5-year-olds and fees for additional hours of attendance and younger children capped at a low rate.[1] Parental fees contribute to overall costs but make up only a small part; the rest comes from tax-based public funding made directly to services. Responsibility for the system rests nationally with the Education Ministry, which issues a national curriculum, and locally

---

1 For example, the maximum monthly cost for a first child is 1,260 krona (114 pounds stirling), and reduces for subsequent children. Arguably, the system lacks 100 percent integration because a period of free attendance does not extend to children below 4 years.

with municipal education departments, which still manage most preschools despite government pressure to increase private providers.

In addition, a number of other European countries are nearly fully integrated, including the three Baltic states and Croatia. They miss full integration because they do not offer an equal entitlement to children under and over 3 years of age (even if guaranteed by law, the reality is that there are insufficient places to guarantee admission for younger children). Germany has recently introduced a universal entitlement to children from 12 months of age and is implementing this guarantee, so it, too, is on the cusp of full integration.

The remaining countries in Europe are still wholly or largely split. Belgium, France and Italy, for example, each have two sectors: one ('childcare') within the welfare system, with separate services for children up to 3 years staffed by childcare workers; the other ('education') within the education system, with services for children from 2½ or 3 years of age staffed by teachers. But a few countries with split systems have begun the process of integration without completing the process, a striking example being England.

The 'New Labour' government, voted into power in 1997, took the first steps towards developing a more integrated system in England (responsibility for early childhood services in other parts of the UK has been devolved to Scotland, Wales and Northern Ireland). Policy making and administrative responsibility were brought together in the national Education Ministry, with daycare services (now commonly referred to as 'childcare services') transferred there from the Health Ministry. A single national inspection system was introduced, with all early childhood services coming under the purview of the schools inspectorate (OFSTED), and a national curriculum emerged, in the prescriptive form of the Early Years Foundation Stage. So by the end of the Labour administration in 2010 all early childhood services were included within a common administrative and regulatory framework.

The integrating process then came to a halt. Nothing was done on the structural dimensions that might be deemed most difficult, not least because of their major economic implications for a system that since the late 1980s has become increasingly reliant on private for-profit childcare services. A universal entitlement to free early childhood education was introduced by the Labour government but remained confined to part-time attendance for 3- and 4-year-olds; a Labour proposal for free provision of early education to 2-year-olds, subsequently implemented by a Conservative-led coalition government (2010–15), was limited to children from lower-income families. However, even for these children a yawning gap remained between the end of high-paid leave, just 6 weeks after birth, and the start of free attendance at early childhood services. Two systems of funding (demand and supply) have continued to run alongside each other, with childcare services heavily dependent on parental fees subsidised in part through a tax credit system; while the early education entitlement for older children is provided free to parents, with public money paid direct to schools that provide nursery classes and to other providers of this entitlement.[2]

Despite efforts to raise the qualification levels of the poorly educated childcare workforce working in day nurseries, playgroups and as childminders, it has remained far less qualified than the far smaller school-based workforce with its graduate teachers. The earnings gap between relatively well-paid school teachers and poorly paid childcare workers has remained as wide as ever. The continuing second class status of childcare workers has been described in a recent study of the workforce:

> The childcare workforce used to be poorly qualified relative to the general workforce, but now there is evidence qualification levels are modestly rising. ... However, childcare workers are not being rewarded for this increase in level of qualification; childcare workers are persistently low paid (on average £6.60 per hour or £10,324 per annum in 2012–14) compared with other occupations (£13.10 per hour or £24,128 per annum in 2012–14). This level of pay is only 10 pence above the 'National Minimum Wage' level and £1.25 below the 'Living Wage for the UK'. Pay is particularly low for childcare workers employed in the private sector (£5.60 per hour compared with £7.80 per hour in the non-private sector, LFS 2012–14).
> (Simon, Owen, & Hollingworth, 2015, p. 3)

Thus, amidst England's early-years provision, a clear fault-line remains between so-called childcare services, dominated by for-profit

---

2  To increase choice and competition, the early education entitlement can be provided not only by schools but by all childcare services that meet certain conditions.

private nurseries, and school-based services, mainly in nursery and reception classes located in primary schools. Integration has stalled.

England makes an interesting comparison with New Zealand. New Zealand began its integration process earlier, with the transfer of responsibility for childcare services in 1986 from the Department of Social Welfare to the Department (now Ministry) of Education. Above all, it has gone further in addressing the really difficult dimensions of integration. It has adopted a common funding formula, applied to all early childhood services, and has also relied primarily on supply rather than demand funding; in other words, supporting services directly rather than subsidising parental fees. Most important of all, New Zealand has tackled the workforce issue head on, with the development of a well-qualified and (relatively) well-paid workforce, based on a graduate early-years teacher, who in 2013 accounted for 76 percent of staff in teacher-led early childhood services (Ministry of Education, 2014). This high level of qualification[3] has been backed by a formula that ensures funding increases for services as they take on more qualified workers, thus encouraging services to employ qualified and registered teachers and provide commensurate pay rates.

While New Zealand addressed the workforce issue from the start, developing and paying for a new graduate professional not only to lead centres but to work directly with children both over and under 3 years, England has totally failed to rise to the challenge. Attempts to improve the qualification levels of the workforce have been, as noted above, modest in ambition, and there has been no funding formula to support enhanced qualification and pay. The result has been a workforce that remains split between a relatively small number of graduate teachers in schools working with 3- and 4-year-olds (and not qualified to work with children under 3 years), and a large and growing body of childcare workers, few of whom have graduate-level qualifications and whose pay remains scandalously low, dependent as it is on what parents are able

---

3 Previous New Zealand governments committed to a goal of a 100 percent graduate teacher workforce, which was subsequently cut back to 80 percent. While this reduced target has been criticised in some quarters, current levels of qualification in New Zealand remain far ahead of anywhere else in the world.

or willing to pay.[4]

Arguably, England has gone further than New Zealand on entitlement, including all 3- and 4-year-olds. Although New Zealand's 20 Hours Free ECE may make attendance for this age group more affordable, and the Government has a target of 98 percent having attended an early childhood education setting before starting school, there is no *entitlement* at any age to a place in early childhood education. Both countries, therefore, are far from providing a universal entitlement from 12 months or the end of well-paid statutory leave. Both countries, too, are a long way off meeting the 'type of provision' criterion of all services being open to all children. Instead, they continue to run a jumble of provision, with different services providing for different groups of children, divisive in effect rather than integrative and inclusive.

In England a new form of integrated provision, Children's Centres, was introduced by the New Labour administration, with the potential to provide holistic services to all children and families. But instead of being developed as a universal service that would eventually replace the existing jumble of provision, it has become just another type of provision, compounding fragmentation. Indeed, far from being the future shape of English provision, Children's Centres today, under a regime of relentless austerity, are withering as funding is cut: centres are closing or reducing the services they offer, and a potentially universal service increasingly targets the use of reducing resources.

Finally, New Zealand has moved far ahead of England conceptually, towards a broad and inclusive understanding of early childhood education as the concept to underpin an integrated early childhood system. As Anne Meade and Val Podmore note:

> The integration of childcare into the Department of Education in New Zealand was preceded by the use of an integrating concept of 'early childhood care and education' (ECCE), for example in the titles of several working groups in the 1980s. Around the time the draft

---

4 The English government has recently introduced a new 'Early Years Teacher', a graduate role to work with children from birth to 5 years. However, this new breed of teacher will not have Qualified Teacher status, and therefore will not have parity with teachers in compulsory education. There is also no goal for the deployment of these new teachers, nor funding to support their widespread deployment and parity of earnings.

version of *Te Whāriki*, [the] early childhood curriculum, was released (1993), 'early childhood education' (ECE) again became the integrating concept and official term as people took for granted that early education involved care as well. Early childhood education continues to be used as the generic term covering the diverse range of types of ECE services in New Zealand. (Meade & Podmore, 2010, p. 32)

So although 'childcare' remains in use in New Zealand, this divisive term—with its narrow association with minding the children of employed parents—has been challenged by an inclusive idea of education in its broadest sense, a concept at the heart of *Te Whāriki*, the early childhood curriculum for all age groups. In England, early childhood services have conceptually become more, not less, divided under the governments that succeeded the New Labour administration, with early childhood services and entitlements increasingly referred to in terms of 'childcare'. The two main policy papers of the Conservative-led coalition government (2010–15) were titled *More Great Childcare* and *More Affordable Childcare* (Department of Education [England] 2013a, b). Jumping on the bandwagon, non-government organisations (NGOs) and parliamentary committees have poured out reports on 'childcare', not one of which addresses the issue of the meaning of and relationship between education and care, or the question of the desirability and feasibility of full integration. But perhaps most striking of all, the Conservative government in 2015 announced a doubling of the free entitlement for 3- and 4-year-olds from 15 to 30 hours a week. However, this additional time is not to be 'early education' for all children, but instead 'a free childcare entitlement' limited to children with employed parents. This targeted measure is being legislated for in a 'Childcare Act'.

## Conclusion

Integrating split early childhood systems to rectify their dysfunctional legacy is important, a major first step in creating an equitable, inclusive and comprehensive public service. Once substantive movement begins on this front, other steps are more readily taken, opening the way to developing an early childhood service that is democratic, innovative and responsive to diversity. Neither England nor New Zealand has fully made this transition, but there is no doubt that

New Zealand has gone further and has more successfully tackled some of the most difficult issues of transition. Substantive movement has begun and democratic, innovative and responsive initiatives have followed, including curriculum and assessment.

As any New Zealander will readily admit, it has not been an untroubled journey, with periods of real progress interspersed with headwinds blowing reform off course (for an overview of recent developments, see Mitchell, 2015); there have been, and still are, 'many challenges and tribulations' (Tesar, 2015, p. 9). To take just two examples, the goal of a totally graduate teacher workforce has not been achieved, while the highly original Centres of Innovation programme, linking academic researchers with innovative practitioners, was closed down by government. Perhaps most disappointing, at least from this outsider's perspective, has been the failure to develop a fully integrated type of provision offering a public, multi-purpose and inclusive service to all children, families and communities. This raises questions about how far a fully integrated early childhood service is compatible with marketisation and for-profit provision.

Yet much has been achieved, more than in England or any other Anglophone country, and the reforms have won New Zealand many admirers, such that the country has become a world leader in early childhood education. How and why this state of affairs has come about is beyond the scope of this chapter. Indeed, it can seem, from the outside at least, little short of miraculous given the immobility of other Anglophone countries and the emergence of reform in New Zealand from a political environment dominated by strong neoliberal sentiments, which elsewhere have proven so unfavourable to integrative reform.

Individuals rarely play a determining role in history, but they can nevertheless be important. That is how New Zealand looks to me: various complex political, social and economic factors created a space for reform, but the form and direction it took depended considerably on the shared vision of a group of formidable and inspiring women. This group not only articulated the vision of an integrated service available as of right for all children, and that addressed the needs of all children, families and communities, but went on to campaign for and help enact that vision, sustaining it during less favourable political conditions.

Anne Smith was part of that group, constantly arguing from a children's rights perspective for an integrated and universal early childhood education service, and defending what has been achieved, not least in her minority report as a member of a government ECE Task Force (2011), challenging the majority who argued for the usual Anglophone pathway of more targeted services. I salute the achievements of Anne and her colleagues in offering hope that alternatives exist and showing they can be realised.

## *References*

Department for Education [England]. (2013a) *More Great Childcare: Raising quality and giving parents more choice.* Retrieved from https://www.gov.uk/government/publications/more-great-childcare-raising-quality-and-giving-parents-more-choice.

Department for Education [England]. (2013b). *More Affordable Childcare.* Retrieved from https://www.gov.uk/government/publications/more-affordable-childcare.

Department of Education [NZ]. (1988). *Education to be more: Report of the Early Childhood Care and Education Working Group.* Wellington: Author. Retrieved from https://www.ucl.ac.uk/childcareinbritain/research-outputs/documents/Childcare-In-Britain-WEB.pdf

Kaga, Y., Bennett, J., & Moss, P. (2010). *Caring and learning together: Cross-national research on the integration of ECCE within education.* Paris: UNESCO. Retrieved from http://www.unesco.org/new/en/education/themes/strengthening-education-systems/early-childhood/coordination-and-integration/study-on-the-integration-of-ecce/

Kahn, A., & Kamerman, S. (1976). *Child-care programs in nine countries: A report prepared for the OECD working party on the role of women in the economy.* Paris: OECD.

Meade, A., & Podmore, V. (2010). *Caring and learning together: A case study of New Zealand.* Paris: UNESCO. Retrieved from http://unesdoc.unesco.org/images/0018/001872/187234e.pdf

Mitchell, L. (2015). Shifting directions in ECEC policy in New Zealand: From a child rights to an interventionist approach. *International Journal of Early Years Education.* doi: 10.1080/09669760.2015.1074557

Ministry of Education. (2014). *Teachers in early childhood education.* Retrieved from https://www.educationcounts.govt.nz/statistics/archived/ece2/ece-indicators/541900

OECD (Organisation for Economic Cooperation and Development). (1974). *Care of children of working parents*. Paris: Author.

Simon, A., Owen, C., & Hollingworth, K., with Rutter, J. (2015) *Provision and use of preschool childcare in Britain*. London, UK: UCL Institute of Education.

Skolverket. (2010). *Curriculum for the preschool: Lpfö 98 Revised 2010*. Stockholm: Skolverket.

Tesar, M. (2015). New Zealand perspectives on early childhood education. *Journal of Pedagogy*, 6(2), 9–20.

# Index

Page numbers in **bold** refer to photographs.

1990 Commemoration Medal 5

access
  to early childhood education and care 3–4, 25, 28, 53–55, 111, 113, 116, 119
  to materials and places 43
Act on Early Childhood Education and Care 2015 (Finland) 41
Action for Children and Youth Aotearoa (ACYA) 50, 53
advocacy vii, viii, 2, 3, 4, 5, 23
  children's rights 28
  by ECEC leaders 91–94
  for infants 25–33
  for social change in early childhood education and care 93–94
  sociocultural approach 25–28
aggression, conflicts and rough-and-tumble play 30
American Orthopsychiatric Association (Ortho) vii, 5
assessment for learning 59–60, 68
  facilitating educational environment, and consistency across span of education 61–63
  feedback and guidance 61, 65, 66, 67–68
  initial capability and performance 64
  monitoring progress over time 60–61
  self-efficacy as desired consequence 63–65
  as a shared process 65–67
Australia 88, 89

Before Five policies 4
behaviour management ix
Bell, Marie 17, 20
Bowlby, John 14, 22
breakfast in an ECEC centre, example of advocacy 91–94
Bronfenbrenner, Urie viii
Burns, Val 17

Caldwell, Bettye 3–4, 21–22
Canada 13–14
capabilities, individual differences 63–64
Care of Children Act 2004
  Section 4(1) 74, 83–84
  Section 6 85
Centres of Innovation 55, 118
child abuse 79
child labour 80–81
child policy ix, x–xi, xii, 3, 6–7, 20
  child poverty 75
  childcare ix, 2–3, 15–17, 21, 22–23, 113, 114, 115
  children's rights 50–51
  early childhood education and care 16–17, 29, 54–55, 91–93, 110, 111, 112–19
  Finland 39–40
  Before Five policies 4
  infants 29, 31, 33
  and research 6
  Swedish preschool 97–98, 99–100
child poverty 75, 80, 99
child protection systems, children's rights in 79–80
childcare

121

*see also* early childhood education and care (ECEC); early childhood education and care centre staff; integrated early childhood systems
  Anne Smith's personal experience 13–15
  *Childcare: Facts, Principles and Problems* (Committee on Women) 21
  Dunedin Community Childcare Association 18, 28
  Dunedin Community Childcare Centre 3, 18–20
  *Early Childhood Educare: The Search for Quality* (video) 4
  effects on children 2, 16, 22, 53–54
  England 111, 113
  enhancement of family life 16, 22
  funding 20, 21, 23, 114, 115
  government policy ix, 2–3, 15–17, 21, 22–23, 113, 114, 115
  origins 110
  and women's rights 2, 15, 53, 97
  *You Can't Afford to be Casual About Child Care* (film) 4, 22
  youngest children 3, 110, 113
childhood, constructed nature 81
childhood studies, university viii
Children's Issues Centre (CIC), University of Otago xii, 4, 26, 28–31, 48, 52
children's participation at school 78–79
children's participation in ECEC 40–41, 44–45
  Finland 41–44
  Hart's ladder model 42, 43
  rights 52, 53–55, 77, 101–02, 116
  Sweden 99, 100–02, 104
  Turja's model 42–43, 44
children's rights 2–3, 7, 48, 72–73, 81
  *see also* United Nations Convention on the Rights of the Child (UNCRC)
  access to ECEC services 3–4, 25, 28, 53–55, 111, 113, 116, 119
  advocacy and research ix–xii, 28
  assessment for learning 59, 65–67, 68
  in child protection systems 79–80
  *Children's Rights: Towards Social Justice* (Smith) 68, 72–73, 81
  within ECEC services 76–77
  within families 74–76
  Finland 37, 38
  to health 80
  high quality, safe and culturally responsive extra-familial environments 86
  infants 26, 27
  participation in ECEC 52, 53–55, 77, 101–02
  at school 4, 77–79
  Sweden 99
  in the workplace 80–81
children's voice ix, 4, 40, 67, 72, 73, 76, 77
*Childrenz Issues* journal 4
Childwatch International ix
citizenship, children's ix, x–xi, 4, 7
Combined Early Childhood Union of Aotearoa 4
Committee on Women, *Childcare: Facts, Principles and Problems* 21
community childcare 16
Companion of the New Zealand Order of Merit 5

competencies, assessment 61, 62
competencies for learning 39
Conference on Women in Social and Economic Development, 1976 22–23
continuous assessment 66
contradictions in ECEC centres 90–93
Crimes Act 1961, Section 59 5, 51
Crimes (Substituted Section 59) Amendment Act 2007 52
cultural-historical activity theory (CHAT) 88, 89
curriculum
 England 113
 Finland 39
 integrated early childhood systems 111
 *New Zealand Curriculum* 62
 Swedish preschool 97, 99, 101, 102–03, 111–12
 *Te Whāriki* 26, 28–29, 54, 61–63, 65, 117

Davies, Sonja 17, 21
daycare *see* childcare
Department of Education
 childcare administration 3, 23, 115, 116
 kindergarten and playcentre support 13
developmental psychology viii
developmental work research (DWR) 89–93
digital environments 86
discrimination
 children at school 77, 78
 families, and children within families 74
 women 15
division of labour in ECEC centres 89. 90
divorce and family changes 4, 76
Dunedin Collective for Women 18
Dunedin Community Childcare Association 18, 28
Dunedin Community Childcare Centre 3, 18–20
Dunedin Multidisciplinary Health and Development Study 73

*Early Childhood Care and Education* (State Services Commission) 23
Early Childhood Care and Education Working Group 110
Early Childhood Conventions 4, 16
*Early Childhood Educare: The Search for Quality* (video) 4
early childhood education and care (ECEC)
 *see also* childcare; children's participation in ECEC; infants in early childhood education; integrated early childhood systems; kindergartens; playcentres; Swedish preschool system
 children's experiences 6–7, 25, 27, 29, 31–32
 children's rights to ECEC 3–4, 25, 28, 53–55, 111, 113, 116, 119
 children's rights within ECEC 76–77, 116
 curriculum, *Te Whāriki* 26, 28–29, 54, 61–63, 65, 115
 funding 115
 government policy 16–17, 29, 54–55, 91–93, 110, 112–19

group size 30, 32, 44, 53, 99, 100–01, 103
holistic approach 40, 61, 62, 109, 111–12, 116
quality 2, 3, 4, 6, 14, 20, 28–30, 32, 33, 54–55, 67, 77, 99, 100, 101, 104
role in levelling socioeconomic differences 38
socioeconomic importance 97, 104
standards 32–33
targeted provision 54–55
early childhood education and care (ECEC), Finland 37–38
children's participation 41–44
context 38–39
first phase of lifelong learning path 37–38
integrated education and care 39–41
early childhood education and care centre staff
see also leaders of early childhood education and care centres
children's participation 40, 41–44
conditions of work 30–31
contradictions 90–93
education and training 17, 18, 20, 29, 30, 32, 33, 53, 54, 55, 97, 99, 100, 109, 114, 115, 116, 118
Finland 41–44
influence on infants and children 26, 29, 30, 68, 104
intervention in aggression, conflicts and rough-and-tumble play 30
pay 20, 29, 114, 115–16
pedagogical challenges 30, 42, 43, 44, 99, 102–03
ratios to children 30, 32, 33, 44, 99, 103
relationships and interactions with children 30, 31–32, 33, 41–44, 68, 96–97, 103, 104
research findings 29
rules, division of labour, tools and objects of activity 89–91
standards 32–33
Sweden 96–97, 99, 100, 102–03
teacher–infant joint attention 30
Early Childhood Education Centres of Innovation 55, 118
*Early Years Learning Framework* (Australian Department of Education, Employment and Workplace Relations) 88
"educare" 3, 4, 40
Education and the Equality of the Sexes Conference, 1975 17
Education Review Office 54
*Education to be More* (Department of Education) 110
emotional states 43
England
Children's Centres 116
progress toward an integrated early childhood system 113–18

families
see also parents
and assessments 59, 61
benefits of childcare and early childhood education 16, 22, 23, 28, 33, 53
children's rights within 74–76
discrimination 74
divorce and family changes 4, 76
Flynn, Jim, *Does Your Family Make You Smarter?* 74

influence on learning and
    development 55, 67, 73
and physical punishment 51
state intervention 79–80, 110
supplying breakfast for children to
    eat in an ECEC centre 91–94
voices 61, 65
Family Court 76
feedback, in assessment 61, 65, 66,
    67–68
fees paid for early childhood
    services 98, 112, 114, 115–16
feminism 15, 19, 20, 21, 53
    *see also* women's rights
Finland *see* early childhood education
    and care (ECEC), Finland
Flynn, Jim, *Does Your Family Make
    You Smarter?* 74
formative assessment 66, 68
foster parents 79–80
Fröebel, Friedrich 39
Fryer, Norah 17–18

government policy *see* child policy

Hart's ladder model of children's
    participation 42, 43
Head Start (USA) 3, 22
health, children's rights 80
Hubbard, Pat 18, 20, 21

immigrant children in ECEC,
    Sweden 98, 99, 100, 101
inclusion 76
inequality
    split systems 110
    Swedish preschool system 99–100
infants in early childhood education
    and care 3, 26–28, 32–33, 113

access to qualified teachers 29, 30,
    32–33, 53, 100, 114, 115–16
aggression, conflicts and rough-
    and-tumble play 30
childcare 3, 110, 113
Children's Issues Centre
    research 28–31
current research 31–32
interpersonal experiences 31–32
rights 33
standards 32–33
teacher–infant joint attention 30
integrated early childhood
    systems 109–10, 117–18
conceptual integration 111–12
criteria 111
Europe 112–15
Finland 39–41
New Zealand 115–19
open to all children 111
from split to integrated
    systems 110–12
Sweden 111–13
International Women's Year, 1975 15–
    18, 20
International Year of the Child,
    1979 49
ipsative assessment 60–61

Jebb, Eglantyne 49

Katz, Lilian 4
kindergartens 13, 14, 16, 23, 39, 97,
    110

Labour and Labour-led
    governments 23, 54
Langer Award vii, 5
leaders of early childhood education

and care centres 86–87, 94
advocacy for social change in early childhood education and care 93–94
Australian settings 88
developing capacity 88–91
example of advocacy 91–93
leadership as taking action for children 87–88

learning
*see also* assessment for learning
identities 60, 63, 77
individual differences in capability 63–64
motivation 60, 61, 63, 64, 67
learning community xi–xii
Learning in the Making study 68
learning stories 63
learning-to-learn skills 38, 39
Lee, Wendy 17
Levitt, Phyllis 18
lifelong learning 39
local government
participation by young people 5
and problem of children eating breakfast at an ECEC centre 91–94

Marion Langer Award vii, 5
McDonald, Geraldine 17, 21, 23
Meade, Anne 17, 21
mentoring, in early childhood services 88
Morris, Beverley 17
motivation for ongoing learning 60, 61, 63, 64, 67

National and National-led governments 23, 54

National Council of Women 15
National Standards 60, 62
New Zealand Association of Child Care Centres (NZACCC) 17–18, 21, 22
*New Zealand Curriculum* 62
Noonan, Rosslyn 15, 17, 21
normative assessment 60

OECD (Organisation for Economic Co-operation and Development) 3, 26, 33, 99, 110

parents
*see also* families
choice of early childhood care and education 29
communication of research findings ix
fees paid for early childhood services 98, 112, 114, 115–16
foster parents 79–80
influence on progress in learning and development 67
involvement in early childhood education and care 19, 20, 44–45, 99, 101–02
satisfaction with quality 29
satisfaction with Swedish preschool 98
supplying breakfast for children to eat in an ECEC centre 91–94
parent–staff communications 3
participation *see* children's participation at school; children's participation in ECEC
peer observations and feedback in learning 66–67
perseverance 64

physical punishment, abolition ix, 51–52, 72, 75–76
play 30, 38, 102, 103, 110
playcentres 13, 16, 23
policy *see* child policy
portfolios, in assessment 61, 89
poverty, children 75, 80, 99
Prime Minister's Conference on Women in Social and Economic Development 21

Renwick, William 16–17
research
    attributes of effective researchers x–xii
    based on Dunedin Community Childcare Centre 20
    children's experiences in day-care settings 3
    Children's Issues Centre research on quality ECEC for infants 28–31
    children's participation in ECEC 40–41
    children's rights ix–xii, 28
    children's voice 4, 40
    current research on infants in ECEC 31–32
    developmental work research (DWR) 89–93
    discipline and guidance of children 52, 76
    interplay with child policy 6, 14
    Learning in the Making study 68
    pedagogical approaches to children's learning and development 96–97
    quality childcare 14, 16, 25–26
    quality experiences in early childhood 14

resilience 53, 64, 79
rights *see* children's rights; women's rights
Royal Society of New Zealand fellowship 5

Sadler, Royce 65
Save the Children International Union 49
school, children's rights 4, 77–79
    exclusion 77–78
    participation 78–79
self-assessment 65–66
self-efficacy 60, 63–65
sex differences in children's activities 3
sex-role stereotyping 3, 20
Smith, Anne B.
    awards vii, 5
    career and achievements viii, ix, xi–xii, 2–5
    photographs **12, 19**
Smith, Catherine **12**
Smith, John **12**, 13, 14
Smith, Juliet **12**
social justice xii, 27, 72–73, 76, 77, 81
    assessment for learning 59, 68
    *Children's Rights: Towards Social Justice* (Smith) 68, 72–73, 81
split early childhood systems
    Europe 113
    from split to integrated systems 110–12
standards for early childhood education services 32–33
standards-based assessment 60
state care of children 79–80
State Service Commission, *Early Childhood Care and Education* 23
Stevens, Ewing 19, **19**

Stonehouse, Anne 4
subjects, assessing 61, 62, 63
Sustained Development Goals (United Nations) 104
Swedish National Agency for Education 97, 98, 100, 102
Swedish preschool system 96, 103–04, 111–13
   curriculum 97, 99, 101, 102–03, 111–12
   fees 98, 112
   forty years of statutory preschool 97–98
   increase in inequality 99–100
   international rankings 99
   research context 96–97
   situation today 98

targeted provision of ECEC 54–55
Te Whāriki 26, 28–29, 54, 61–63, 65, 117
teachers *see* early childhood education and care centre staff; leaders of early childhood education and care centres
trust in person offering guidance 67
Turja's model of children's participation 42–43, 44

UNESCO 110–11
United Nations Committee on the Rights of the Child 50–51
   position on participation of children in ECEC 53
   position on physical punishment 51–52, 75
United Nations Convention on the Rights of the Child (UNCRC) 27, 28, 31, 37, 40, 44, 48, 54, 55, 65, 77, 79, 80, 81
   Article 3 83
   Article 6.2 84
   Article 12 84–85
   Article 19 84
   framework for family life of children 74–76
   *General Comment No. 7* (2005) 53
   genesis 49–50
   optional protocols 50
   reporting process 50–51
United Nations Sustained Development Goals 104
United Women's Convention, 1975 15
University of Otago 2, 13
   Children's Issues Centre (CIC) xii, 4, 26, 28–31, 48, 52
   crèche 14
   Department of Education 14
University of Oulu, Finland, honorary doctorate 5

Victorian Maternal and Child Health Services 80
Vygotsky, Lev 30, 40, 96

welfare services viii, 13, 23, 37, 94, 110, 113, 115
women's rights 2, 3, 15, 97
   *see also* feminism
workforce, children in 80–81

*You Can't Afford to be Casual About Child Care* (film) 4, 22

www.ingramcontent.com/pod-product-compliance
Lightning Source LLC
Chambersburg PA
CBHW060301240426
43661CB00060B/2858